PRAISE
Fractured Souls & Sp

MW00354957

This book shares the powerful healing journey of a woman who lived through horrific abuse as a child and teen. It provides an example of how, even though challenging beyond what most of us can ever imagine, an adult who seeks help from a gifted mental health expert can emerge with peace, hope, and wholeness. Dr. Kane's writings provide an example of how a hallowed relationship between client and therapist can transform souls. This is a great contribution to the mental health field!

—Dr. Susan R. Madsen
Author, speaker, and scholar

A poignant but powerful story of hurt, hope, and healing, *Fractured Souls and Splintered Memories* shines a beautiful light on the process of opening up and revealing hurt and need in a way that draws us in and helps us examine the hurt and need in our own lives. It is enlightening to read the path of trust and love that was established with Michelle's therapist that gave her the safety and support she needed to fully open and reveal her past and present. *Fractured Souls* gives us all permission to seek out and find the safety we need to open our own boxes—revealing our need for healing but then giving room to fill each box with healing and hope for the future. Truly, a tender read for us all.

—Merrilee Browne Boyack
Author, speaker, and lawyer

In this age of turmoil and unrest, there is an increasing need for careful guidance and direction to ease the pain of those who have suffered trauma in their lives. This book recounts a history of healing through the analytical expertise of a professionally trained counselor whose understanding and patience brings healing to the life of a troubled soul. Although the book deals with one set of circumstances, the principles and practices identified can be applied in varying circumstances. One with challenging circumstances can personally benefit from reading and pondering the techniques described in this book. The author is skilled in guiding her clients to determine solutions that will be of lasting benefit. The author writes from an extensive history of counseling. In addition to her academic qualifications, she is known for her compassion and understanding.

—Elaine L. Jack
Twelfth Relief Society General President of
The Church of Jesus Christ of Latter-day Saints, 1990–97

Fractured Souls

&

Splintered

Memories

UNLOCKING the "Boxes" of Trauma

CHRISTY P. KANE, PsyD, CMHC

PLAIN SIGHT PUBLISHING
An imprint of Cedar Fort, Inc.
Springville, Utah

© 2021 Christy Kane
All rights reserved.

No part of this book may be reproduced in any form whatsoever, whether by graphic, visual, electronic, film, microfilm, tape recording, or any other means, without prior written permission of the publisher, except in the case of brief passages embodied in critical reviews and articles.

This is not an official publication of The Church of Jesus Christ of Latter-day Saints. The opinions and views expressed herein belong solely to the author and do not necessarily represent the opinions or views of Cedar Fort, Inc. Permission for the use of sources, graphics, and photos is also solely the responsibility of the author.

ISBN 13: 978-1-4621-4032-9

Published by Plain Sight Publishing, an imprint of Cedar Fort, Inc.
2373 W. 700 S., Springville, UT 84663
Distributed by Cedar Fort, Inc., www.cedarfort.com

Library of Congress Control Number: 2021932773

Cover design by Shawnda T. Craig
Cover design © 2021 Cedar Fort, Inc.

Printed in the United States of America

10 9 8 7 6 5 4 3 2 1

Printed on acid-free paper

CONTENTS

Contents

PROLOGUE 1

ONE OF THE SACRED OFFERINGS OF THERAPY, WHICH IS PROTECTED BY A CODE of ethics, is the gift of confidentiality. As a mental health expert, I have written this book to provide readers with an intimate look into the therapeutic process of healing while protecting the identity of the client, who I will refer to as Michelle Chambers, and the identity of the psychologist, who I will refer to as Dr. Natalie Stachowski. To accomplish this objective, I share a mental-health healing journey in which two amazing individuals participated. By keeping their identities confidential, I am able to allow both rawness and vulnerability as I share a story of transformation.

In this book, you will discover the resiliency of the human soul as it is protected and shepherded by a gifted mental health professional. To complement the story, I include commentary that adds insight and clarification at the beginning of each chapter.

The ultimate aim of this book is not to highlight the darkness that Michelle went through but to emphasize the truth—that healing is possible, if those who seek it are dedicated to the work required to obtain this gift in their own way and at their own time, just as you will see Michelle did.

—Dr. Christy P. Kane, PsyD, PhD, CMHC

PROLOGUE 2

THE THERAPIST'S PATH IS AS VARIED AS THE PEOPLE WHO SEEK OUR HELP. We embark on a journey with a new client, hoping that we can be of some help in alleviating their pain, promoting healing from past hurts, or simply supporting them through some storm they must weather. Many times, we are able to fulfill one or more of these functions. Our client's pain is reduced, or they reach some resolution to a difficult chapter from their past. Or, if we cannot provide them with tools to reduce their emotional pain, we accompany them through the storm so that even if the pain cannot be avoided, they do not have to face it alone.

Other times, we question whether we have helped our client at all. Perhaps the seeker has come wanting only sympathy and support for their own misguided thinking, or even some form of forgiveness for hurt they have caused others. Other times, they have been coerced into therapy by a third party, the court system or an exasperated partner who has threatened to leave the relationship if they do not seek help. Sometimes these clients are helped in spite of themselves, discovering the power of self-reflection and choosing to embark on an inner quest to heal. Many others, however, "put in their time" but do not engage in the work necessary to truly change and grow.

Once in a while, however, therapy is a truly sacred journey. The seeker arrives in our office at just the right time, and we are just the right person to help them at whatever crossroads they have found themselves. At these times, it does not seem a coincidence that this client has walked into this particular therapist's office. Rather, it is as if a connection already exists, and the path they are about to embark on together is already marked. This does not mean the path is easy, and, in fact, such journeys are often the most demanding and daunting that the therapist will take. But, if they are very fortunate, their client will grow to trust them enough to persist, to follow the path even when the terrain is daunting and the cliffs they must traverse strike terror, not comfort.

The therapist on a journey such as this will don the cloak of a sage or, at times a magician, hoping and even praying along the way that their magic is more than simply smoke and mirrors, and will be strong enough for the task. At its best, the therapeutic journey is one of growth and healing for the therapist as well as their client. This is the story of such a journey.

—Dr. Natalie Stachowski

CHAPTER 1

Even in Darkness There Will Be Light

Even in darkness, there will be light if one is willing to step forward for the view.

MICHELLE SITS ON HER CABIN PORCH IN A WOODEN ROCKING CHAIR WRAPPED in her quilt of healing, enjoying a cup of Earl Gray tea and reflecting why she loves this quilt so much as her mind briefly flashes on another image . . . . a little child sitting alone in the corner of an old trailer in disrepair. It is winter, and she is draped in a threadbare blanket yearning for warmth. Michelle thinks of what a long journey it has been to where she is now and smiles. She picks up her pen and begins to write:

> For a long time, I have thought about sharing my story, yet hesitated to do so. I didn't want to offend those closest to me. I didn't want anyone to refer to me as that abused child, that broken woman seeking to be loved while longing for wholeness never able to taste either. I didn't want to harm the relationship my children shared with my extended family, and I was concerned that others might judge me and consider my experience too stained. After much heartfelt interpersonal conversation and with a desire to help others learn from my experience, I made the choice to entrust Dr. Kane with the telling of mine and Dr. Natalie's journey. Now that I have shared my story with Dr. Kane, I am relatively confident my words would have been dark if I had shared my story prior to completing my personal journey of healing.

This journey was a passage that, for me, involved climbing mountains, experiencing spiritual direction, commencing difficult conversations, discovering truths, unlocking boxes, painting unconscious thoughts, and embracing a child. Toward the end of this most complex and enlightening spiritual pilgrimage, I allowed myself to trust that I would finally and honestly know love, feel love, and be loved by those around me—in particular by the only people who would genuinely know my unlit boxes.

As you read Dr. Kane's thoughts regarding my therapy, instead of focusing on events of abuse, neglect, and anguish, focus on gaining a greater understanding of the therapeutic healing process. Why such a journey should be engaged in by humans and how such a journey, if taken at the right time with the right therapist, can be life altering. There are so many hurting in this world needlessly. So many of us know loved ones who suffer from traumas that lead to depression, anxiety, and at times suicide ideation. Learn from this book for yourself and for others that therapy is a sacred gift, not a mysterious threat.

Also understand that healing from abuse and how abuse is processed is as diverse as the abused person. For some it is a journey of moving away from emotional over-control and compartmentalization to the safety of emotional release, emotional expression, and allowing one's self to feel emotions, which was my journey. For others it is the process of learning to set boundaries and gain emotional control. Far too often abuse survivors are stereotyped as a broken person, and yet those who appeared more put together can also be victims of abuse who coped by strong emotional defense mechanisms, like compartmentalization. Also please understand that the journey to healing needs to be taken with the right person, at the right time, and in the right way, sustained through the healing power of the Atonement of Jesus Christ.

—Michelle Chambers, PhD

CHAPTER 2

In Reflection

True healing is attained as the balm of Gilead is skillfully applied by one who has dedicated his or her life to lift, disentangle, encourage, and guide to wholeness those whose childhood experiences created fractured souls and splintered memories. Ultimate healing comes through the purifying power of the Atonement of Jesus Christ.

"Did it really take eighteen months to get here? Wow, I can't believe we have made it to the close. Thank you, God. This was so not easy, to say the least, but I know I have changed. There are no more secrets," Michelle said to herself as she drove away from Dr. Natalie's office for the last time.

Michelle's final session with Dr. Natalie had just ended, and as she left Dr. Natalie's office and drove home, she was not exactly sure what to feel. Part of her was at peace, knowing a complicated, challenging, intimate healing journey had come to a close. Michelle sensed the foreboding of sadness, understanding that her connection with Dr. Natalie, the only individual she ever completely accepted into her life, was changing. Tears flowed freely as her heart whispered tender expressions of appreciation and salutation.

As Michelle considered her last session with Dr. Natalie, she perceived that Dr. Natalie scheduled this encounter so she could confirm they were indeed at the end of this part of her healing junction. This session was an opportunity to offer tender good-byes with the recognition that their voyage together had come to an end and that Michelle's healing passage would now move forward as a part of daily living through the love, acceptance, and connection of others. Michelle had a peaceful, deepened understanding that true healing is possible—if the weary traveler is willing to enter the Pool of Bethesda, as directed by a sage who considers it their sacred stewardship to teach, confront, embrace, and encourage toward healing those whose childhood conflicts create fractured souls and splintered memories. Michelle discerned that healing comes as one learns the process of self-love, self-acceptance, self-authenticity, absolute truth, and the purifying power of the Atonement of Jesus Christ.

This session was much different from the ones they had engaged in during the last eighteen months on a weekly, biweekly, or even more frequent basis. Eighteen months is an eternity, considering that in Michelle's first session with Dr. Natalie, she made it thoroughly clear she was consenting to meet only for a few weeks. Michelle firmly believed that addressing her issues would require only a few therapeutic encounters while life continued on as usual. Michelle's mentality was to either get it done and over with or to not embark. Now, at a deeper level, Michelle understands that healing is not about getting it done but involves lifting the soul of an individual toward deeper truths.

At the beginning of Michelle's healing journey, she was still hiding from the truth. Michelle proclaimed statements such as, "My childhood did not affect me, and there is not that much to talk about." But as she continued to engage in therapy, Michelle accepted the truth that her childhood was unfathomable. She didn't accept this truth in two weeks, but she did move at therapeutic lightning speed, considering the depths she descended to and the heights she ascended to with the guiding direction of Dr. Natalie. During their sessions, they cried and laughed together. Michelle stopped evading and allowed her childhood to reside in Dr. Natalie's office, fully exposed and pleading for both understanding and resolve.

As Michelle drove home after her last session, she asked herself and God how she could find the words to unfold the sacred, cathartic journey that she and Dr. Natalie had taken. Michelle knew she desired to verbalize the experience.

So much transpired in Dr. Natalie's office and out of her office, and these events are formidable to narrate. Thus, I'm not sure my writings will adequately portray the intensity of emotions and transformation that both client and counselor experienced. But I do know that the complex process of integral healing occurred, and for the first time in Michelle's life, she knows serenity. The phantoms of her childhood no longer haunt her. Michelle now looks at her past with no regrets, no fear, no denial, no minimization of what happened. She allows responsibility for events of the past to be placed where it belongs. Michelle is not the judge of those whose actions caused harm. They must take their own journey of healing and forgiveness. She is no longer bound to them through guilt. Today, she loves them with boundaries that allow her to have a relationship with some of them while staying emotionally safe and supported.

Today through her role as a mother, an active member of her religious faith, a psychologist, and an individual who completed a personal healing odyssey, Michelle knows that nothing justifies child abuse. Michelle looks forward to the future with purposeful direction, knowing that she is a tenacious and profoundly compassionate individual because of her past and her present.

Yes, Michelle's youth included darkness, which, through the process of therapy and the power of the Atonement, has been overpowered by light. Michelle now understands that during the abuse, she possessed great strengths, such as the power to let go and the capacity to love, even when those you love destroyed innocence and the ability to make it just one more day in an unlit and destructive environment.

Michelle developed great faith in a loving Heavenly Father, an understanding that she is not anyone's judge, and an awareness that she is a survivor. She let go of darkness through the process of accepting the truth regarding her abusive childhood. She drew upon her foundation of faith, knowing that although she felt alone in her youth, she was not alone in her healing journey. Michelle was guided and supported by Dr. Natalie; her best friend, Ivan; Barbara; Joy; and Heavenly Father.

CHAPTER 3

A Child's Question

The journey of healing begins when individuals realize they seek deeper meaning and completeness in life. For the quest to be effective, it needs to be navigated by a sage mental health guide and committed participant.

IN A FEW SHORT DAYS, MICHELLE WOULD CELEBRATE HER FORTY-NINTH BIRTH-day. Life indeed passed by in a blink. At least, most of the time. Today wasn't one of those times. Michelle was seated in her office, irritated with a mental distraction as she attempted to review documents. She kept rereading the same paragraph, unable to fully grasp the content, because thoughts from an earlier conversation with her twenty-year-old son, Casey, were intruding. She pushed the documents aside, slid back from her desk, and proclaimed in a slightly frustrated tone, "Okay, yes, my son is right. So what? Why does it matter that I don't let anyone in completely? Or, better yet, why does it matter at this time in my life? I'm almost forty-nine years old. I'm successful; I have four beautiful children. I enjoy life, and 99.9 percent of the time I'm well pleased with my career, my faith, my activities, and my relationship with my children."

However, as Casey had pointed out, there was always a fragile barrier between Michelle and the rest of the world. Who did this barrier affect? Her kids knew she loved them, and they shared positive relationships. They trusted her. Her friends sensed that no matter what, she would be there for them. Michelle was the person who people called in the middle of the night when they needed help or just needed to talk with someone. She was loyal to a fault, ever willing to help, lift, guide, and support those around her.

Michelle's reflections halted as emotions endeavored to surface. She was also the person who some people considered intimidating when they first met her. She was the person whose counsel was sought, but she wasn't the person who received invitations to a girls' weekend or even to dinner. Michelle was the ever-present advisor with whom people felt comfortable discussing their adversities, but she wasn't the person who was welcomed into the merriments of someone else's life.

Yes, as Casey suggested, Michelle was the person who people believed was as consistent as the stars and as steady as the mountains and who never needed a helping hand or a listening ear. Yet Casey saw through that! This morning, he'd asked Michelle why she never spoke of her childhood. Michelle knew it was his way of saying, "Please, let me in, Mom. I love you. Please trust me."

She hoped her son had overlooked her decision to redirect the conversation. She wasn't sure how to talk about her youth. Michelle thought, "How do I tell my son that as a child I lived in fear; longing to be loved but constantly silenced by shame? How do I say out loud to him what I have not even allowed myself to verbalize in the inner most chambers of my heart? What will my son think of me if I tell him who I really am?"

Michelle wasn't sure she was ready. At moments, she yearned to share her past—it could be lonely being her yet humiliation silenced the child she never wanted anyone to know. On some nights, tears flowed freely when she was in the solitude of her car. Because Michelle hid her tears, they were never acknowledged by others. Michelle lacked the words to explain why she withdrew instead of seeking an embrace when life was hard. She wished she felt others could understand her fears while welcoming her past. Michelle thought, "I have made sure no one would ever know my past that no one would have a reason to judge me, and yet here I sit in my office considering telling one of the most important people in my life; my son. What am I thinking? This is stupid, and yet maybe, perhaps just maybe, I can take the risk. I can finally be free and know completing love." Every time Michelle got close to developing an intimate relationship, she physically and emotionally walked away. Here she was, a mental health professional helping others do what she lacked the courage to do. Michelle knew she had been lonely too long. She decided that it was time to finish the journey she had embarked on many years ago with Dr. Natalie Stachowski.

As Michelle dialed Dr. Natalie's office, she wondered whether Dr. Natalie was even still taking clients. She prayed that if she wasn't, she would at least agree to see her so they could finish what they had started but never completed in Michelle's early twenties. Dr. Natalie didn't answer, so Michelle left a voice mail. After ending the call, Michelle breathed a sigh of relief. "If she calls back, I will discuss whether now is the time to unlock boxes. If she does not call back, then life will move forward as it always has. No, my life is not perfect, but it is good enough."

As she turned back toward the documents on her desk, Michelle wasn't sure which to hope for: a call or silence. Deep within her was a haunting feeling of closed off sadness, making her want Dr. Natalie to call her back. Michelle trusted Dr. Natalie and knew she would not complete the journey with anyone else. Michelle also knew that God knew this. As a therapist herself, Michelle understood that true healing comes at the right time, in the right place, and with the right guide, and Dr. Natalie was the right psychologist for her.

CHAPTER 4

The Returned Call

Therapy is not a process of compulsion but a journey of surrender, as pride yields to the rawness of vulnerability. Vulnerability opens wounded souls to the healing power of love, truth, forgiveness, and acceptance.

A FEW WEEKS AFTER MICHELLE LEFT A MESSAGE FOR DR. NATALIE, THE receptionist returned her call and stated that Dr. Natalie wasn't accepting new clients but would be happy to provide a referral. While still on the phone, Michelle breathed a sigh of relief, yet with conflicting thoughts said to herself, "Okay, this is my answer? I made it very clear to myself and to God that I'd only take this journey with Dr. Natalie. Strange, I really thought she would join me in this journey. I guess now I have confirmation that I'm not supposed to take this journey, yet I was really starting to allow myself to believe it was time. Odd. One more closed door, and yet I really thought Dr. Natalie would see me. Maybe I thought we had more of our connection than she did. Well, thank you, Heavenly Father. I can put this whole stupid idea behind me and move forward."

Then, for reasons that Michelle didn't completely understand—but that God certainly did—Michelle said, "Did you, by any chance, let Dr. Natalie know who is asking for the appointment, or did you just call me back based on established protocol?"

The receptionist was silent, apparently unsure how to respond. Seeking to give her an out, Michelle asked to be connected to Dr. Natalie's voice mail. She informed the receptionist that she would leave Dr. Natalie a message explaining that if she didn't want to see her, then she shouldn't return her phone call. Dr. Natalie's receptionist hesitantly agreed. Michelle found herself waiting, again, feeling both trepidation and hope. Why didn't she just accept no for an answer? In the restrained depths of her soul, Michelle understood why. She wanted to let go of the past, to finally add light into the darkness, to tell Dr. Natalie what she should have told her so many years ago. Michelle longed to feel what she had helped so many clients feel yet did not know how to do so for herself. She wanted to taste healing. She also comprehended, to a minimal degree, that what lie ahead for Dr. Natalie and her would not be a casual excursion.

Together they would identify several buried boxes containing secrets. Was Michelle ready to unbury and open the boxes? If not, she needed to be. Michelle knew that if Dr. Natalie agreed to meet with her, she'd seek to determine whether she was prepared to dig up the boxes and remove the contents.

In my own mental health practice, many clients who entered my office weren't ready to do the work they needed to do. Some started the work and then backed away, unprepared to examine what needed to be considered. They were not ready to experience the deep vulnerability that emotions create. Emotions that open wounds that they might be healed by the power of love, truth, forgiveness, and acceptance. Michelle wanted to make sure she was not one of those clients.

"Hi, Dr. Stachowski, it's Michelle Chambers. I am not sure if you remember me or not, but a long time ago you and I visited for a brief period. I was hoping that you might be open to seeing me again. I know you are not taking any new clients, but I was really hoping you might make an exception for me. If not, I completely understand. Please call me back if an exception is possible. If not, then I'll wish you well and hope that all is going great in your life."

Several days later, Michelle received a phone call from Dr. Natalie's office. To her pleasant surprise, she heard Dr. Natalie's voice. "I received your message, and I'm honored that you want to see me again. I'm so sorry, but I am no longer taking any new therapy clients. I'm happy to make a referral."

Michelle's heart sank. This was not the answer she had been silently pleading for. "No, thank you, Dr. Natalie. Either I'll see you or I won't see anyone. You are the person I trust."

Due to their previous short journey together and the connection they felt those many years ago, Dr. Natalie, knowing Michelle had not yet completed her healing journey and that she might return, noted, "Michelle, I figured that would be your reply. I do have an opening this Friday, October 7, at 4:00 p.m. Will that work for you?"

"I'll make that work. Thank you, Dr. Natalie. I promise this journey will not take very many sessions."

"You're very welcome. It will be nice to see you again. See you Friday."

The phone disconnected, and for a long time, Michelle sat in silence, staring at the receiver with multiple voices running through her head. *What are you doing?* the strongest voice repeatedly asked. Michelle valued Dr. Natalie's time and didn't want to waste it—or hers, for that matter. If she was going to keep the appointment, Michelle knew she needed to be committed to the exploration. Was she? Was she ready to share with Dr. Natalie her boxes—boxes that contained darkness she had never told anyone?

"I sure hope I can do this. I would rather not start than start and fail. I guess time will tell. I have helped so many clients take the journey that lies before me, but it feels so different knowing its mine to take. This will be harder than I thought. Breathe, Michelle, just breathe. You can always back out," Michelle said out loud in the deafening silence of her car.

The next week, Michelle engaged in soul searching meditation and prayer, wondering if she was really committed to go all the way, while seeking for spiritual confirmation regarding her decision to start individual psychotherapy. Was now the right time in her life? How would her counseling sessions affect others, in particular her current clients? Did she genuinely comprehend the pilgrimage ahead? For as long as Michelle could remember, she had considered herself a competent and self-reliant individual. Still, the thought of the impending undertaking left her with limited confidence.

Michelle did, however, know that if anyone could guide her through this crusade, it was Dr. Natalie. She had the right expertise, knowledge, respect for Michelle's beliefs, and skill set. Michelle decided not to cancel the appointment. "One therapy session—that's all I have pledged to at the moment. It couldn't hurt, right?" Michelle also knew that the next few days would be filled with limited sleep as she prepared herself to take the long-awaited journey. "Well, what is that old saying that which does not kill us only makes us stronger? I am not sure if this will make me stronger or if it will finally allow me to kill my past. I guess time will tell," thought Michelle. "Time will tell."

CHAPTER 5

The First Appointment

Many years before I decided to major in the field of mental health, I asked an individual whom I admired why she chose to become a psychologist, to which she responded, "People have to go through many difficult things in life but should not have to go through them alone." Her comment directed my path toward the field of mental health.

MICHELLE SPENT MOST WORKDAYS IN BACK-TO-BACK MEETINGS, WHICH demanded a lot of mental focus and executive decision-making. However, on the morning of October 7, she struggled to concentrate as the voices in her head decided to conduct a full judicial review of whether she should or should not keep her 4:00 p.m. appointment with Dr. Natalie. Michelle found herself distracted by the cacophony of convincing arguments offered by the defense and the prosecution. "Enough already. Just stop. I have not even opened a single box, and already I feel like I am going crazy. I just need to get out of this office. I cannot believe I am going to do this. What was I thinking?" Michelle moaned to the voices in her head.

In total frustration, Michelle requested that her receptionist cancel the rest of her meetings for the day. Michelle's petition was accepted with dismay and an inquiry: "Are you feeling sick?" The question was understandable because Michelle rarely made such a request. She explained, "No, I am fine. I just need to redirect my thoughts." Michelle left the office and headed to her favorite tea shop. A change of scenery and a warm cup of chai tea would silence the voices in her head and help her to recenter.

After arriving at the Tea House, Michelle selected a somewhat secluded seat and ordered a fantastic cup of blueberry chai tea with a hint of honey. She closed her eyes and attempted to concentrate on her breathing. Michelle felt limited relief.

The cavalcade of arguments returned for a final defense. "You are a mental health professional who is publicly recognized and has dedicated much of your life to helping others heal from scars and move toward the lives they desire. How will it work for you, a psychologist, to see another psychologist for therapy? Are you out of your mind? You don't have the time to do this. It's not too late to back out. Why are you wanting to take this journey now after all these years?"

Michelle wanted to let go of the idea. A part of her needed to walk away. She desired to go back to her office, pack her schedule tighter than ever before, and run even faster. Michelle was a good runner, even if the only running she did involved running away from emotions. Running felt safe. Running for the last thirty-one years had helped Michelle stay safe and emotionally protected, or at least that is what she thought it did.

Michelle ordered one more cup of tea, this one to go. She noted the clock on the wall, which drew her back from her mental arguments to the reality that it was 3:15 p.m. If she was going to keep her appointment, she had better begin her drive. As Michelle pulled into the parking lot next to Dr. Natalie's office, her thoughts flashed back to 1992 when she, as a young woman, nervously waited to meet with a mental health professional (Dr. Natalie) for the first time. She was only going then because it was a requirement of her doctorate program. Michelle's mental health doctorate program required students to participate in their own personal therapy sessions in order to have a deeper insight into the clinical world thereby offering, soon to be clinicians, empathy not just sympathy for the therapeutic process. Those sessions in 1992 scratched the surface of her childhood and ended when Dr. Natalie suggested that more vulnerability on Michelle's part might lead to greater healing.

How different would Michelle's current appointment be if she had risked vulnerability and talked with Dr. Natalie in 1992 regarding their approaching dialogue? Michelle was relatively certain she wasn't ready then to address her past. She hoped she was now. Michelle ascended the stairs and chose the office chair farthest from Dr. Natalie's closed door, relieved that no one else was in the waiting room. After a few moments, Dr. Natalie opened her door, gave Michelle a warm welcome, and invited her in. Many years ago, as Michelle had walked into Dr. Natalie's office, she sat on the couch opposite of where she was seated now and had felt peace. Today, Michelle felt both apprehensive and vulnerable as she shifted in her seat with her heart racing and shallow breathing, and avoided Dr. Natalie's gaze.

Lucky for Michelle, her session started with a bit of catching up. She and Dr. Natalie covered the directions their lives had taken after their last meeting, more than twenty-five years before. As they talked, the voices in Michelle's head quieted and her emotional turmoil decreased. Michelle once again felt connected to Dr. Natalie, this amazing woman, and knew that in her office she would once again find safety. After all, it was Dr. Natalie, without judgment, with sincere interest, who offered tenderness, time, and keen insight. She desired Michelle to do far more than complete a PhD program requirement, and it was Dr. Natalie who agreed to see Michelle as part of her PhD program. That agreement had opened the door for Michelle to share more than simple day to day happenings of life because there was something about Dr. Natalie that Michelle trusted. Perhaps it was because Dr. Natalie was highly recognized in her field and Michelle valued expertise, or perhaps even way back then Michelle felt Dr. Natalie's deep concern for her and a desire for her to know complete healing, not merely office time in the completion of a doctoral program requirement.

With formalities out of the way, Dr. Natalie addressed the elephant in the room. "So, Michelle, what brings you back to my office? I can't help but think that you'd rather be anyplace but here. My sense is that we did some really important work together the last time you were here, but there was a lot left unsaid. I am guessing that you are here because you're ready to take the next step on what will be a difficult journey."

"Yes, that is the reason I am here, and yes, I know Dr. Natalie, I get it will be hard, and I am praying I am ready. Part of me thinks I am and I also know there is another part of that just wants to bolt and never look back, but I know it is the right time and I trust you."

"Thank you for your trust. It means a lot to me. I hope this time we can get to the end of the journey."

"Agreed."

With a few more directed words, Dr. Natalie and Michelle decided that the appropriate course was to move forward. Dr. Natalie then invited Michelle to explain why she was back in her office after all these years and what she hoped to accomplish.

Michelle breathed deeply and then sat in silence for a moment, petitioning her Heavenly Father for the courage to confess what needed to be removed from the blackness of her childhood. Many years ago, Dr. Natalie and Michelle had discussed her childhood at a surface level because Michelle wasn't ready to acknowledge truth or to divulge wrongdoing. Michelle never wanted anyone to know about her childhood, and she never wanted to hurt anyone. She feared (even though she knew as a therapist her thoughts were irrational but that as a client, they were real) that her past, if known, would persuade people to see her as damaged. They would consider Michelle as broken, not the successful woman who now sat in Dr. Natalie's office. Seated there, Michelle decided that if she was to know complete peace, love, and acceptance, then she had to take the risk and trust that Dr. Natalie would still respect her after she brought it all into the light.

More important than Dr. Natalie's respect, Michelle needed to learn to believe in herself. For longer than she could remember, self-derogatory thoughts constantly ran through her mind: "People are going to discover who you are and that you're a fraud. They'll know you're not who they thought you were. One of these days, they'll all know how appalling you actually are. No matter how successful you are you are nothing but a fraud."

Shifting her gaze from the floor to Dr. Natalie, Michelle said, "I think it is time to take the journey we started many years ago regarding my childhood. I pray I am ready, or at least I hope I am ready, to unlock boxes, disclose secrets, and explore all that we decide together that needs exploration so that I can finally be free of the phantoms that haunt me, and know peace."

Dr. Natalie smiled and said, "I have hoped that someday you would return to finish the work we had not completed, and I'm thankful you trust me enough to be the person who helps you finishes your journey." Before concluding the session, Dr. Natalie and Michelle set appointments for the next several weeks. Michelle still firmly believed that she could achieve therapeutic healing quickly.

Dr. Natalie and Michelle offered warm goodbyes, and then Michelle thanked Dr. Natalie for agreeing to guide her. She believed that God wanted Dr. Natalie to take this journey with her, and Dr. Natalie acknowledged the same belief during a later session. Michelle also believed that Dr. Natalie's life, not just hers, would change in the process. Time would tell whether this belief would turn into reality.

CHAPTER 6

How to Begin

God's crowning gift to His children is the power of feelings and emotions. It is imperative to understand that feelings and emotions are never wrong. Rather, the actions people engage in based on their feelings and emotions can be wrong. Allow yourself to feel your anger, and then act through love. Even anger can be expressed in love.

DURING MICHELLE'S FIRST SET OF APPOINTMENTS WITH DR. NATALIE twenty-five years earlier, Dr. Natalie gave her a homework assignment to write about her childhood. In completing the assignment, Michelle shared limited information and left out her emotions. After Dr. Natalie read the information, she compared Michelle's writing to black icicles on white paper. Basically, Michelle had handed her a laundry list.

Today, as Michelle arrived for her appointment with Dr. Natalie, she needed to find the pathway to not only discuss what happened in her childhood but also to take steps toward describing her emotions regarding the events. If Michelle couldn't take these first steps, then she would be merely repeating the process from many years ago, with the same limited results.

In this session, Michelle needed to convey to the person she trusted, Dr. Natalie, about her childhood experiences with emotional presence. This process of disclosure would help Michelle release shame and doubt. From Michelle's prior therapy sessions, Dr. Natalie knew the following facts: Michelle had experienced some neglect and abuse as a child. Michelle did not have a strong relationship with her parents, but she was complimentary toward them. Michelle tended to blame herself for the physical and emotional abuse her mother directed toward her. Michelle had also been sexually abused but was unwilling to reveal much on this topic.

Michelle needed to expose the dark memories that she had been running from since her youth, but how could she? Michelle wanted to share her feelings, but she had boxed up the darkness the day she left her parents' home, locked the boxes, buried them in the earth, and then had thrown away the key, vowing she would never unearth and unlock the boxes. The locks seemed unbreakable.

Michelle desperately wanted people to believe that she had had a normal childhood and a normal family. If people believed she had a normal family, then all the guilt, shame, and secrets buried in her head and heart could be kept in the dark. A normal family to Michelle meant normal judgment and normal acceptance. Yet, nothing could be further from the truth. Today, with Dr. Natalie's careful guidance, Michelle would start untelling what she had always told people regarding her childhood; she would disclose the truth. Michelle believed that, as noted in John 8:32, the truth makes one free. Therapy was not going to be easy for her—or for Dr. Natalie—but it was time to take the journey, and they both knew it.

After Michelle sat on the couch in Dr. Natalie's office, Dr. Natalie asked two questions: "Michelle, how have you been feeling since your decision to return to therapy? How did you decide to return to therapy at this time in your life?"

Instead of saying what Michelle usually told people— "I am great; nothing is wrong"—she admitted, "I am struggling. I am finding it difficult to sleep, and my emotions feel out of control. One second I want to yell in anger, and the next second I want to sit down and cry. Yet, something is inhibiting me from doing either and it is very frustrating. I am seriously questioning my decision to return to therapy. I am far more comfortable helping others take this journey than taking it myself. Not so easy, but then we both know that."

"Can you tell me about the anger? Let's talk about what's causing these feelings."

Michelle wanted to say, "Because I made this stupid decision to return to therapy. I should've left things well enough alone." Instead of surrendering to her frustration or reverting back to her protective "I have it all together" facade, Michelle acknowledged in a hushed voice, "Because, Dr. Natalie, there are some things I need to tell you. I just do not know how to start. Things I have spent my whole life running from, items that I fear if given a voice such vocalization will destroy me."

Dr. Natalie responded, "Thank you, Michelle, I know there are things you need to share with me, and I am grateful you have found the courage and insight to return. I knew that during our last meeting. In fact, I've known it for a long time. Please remember that this is not a race and we can take time to go through this. I know you want to get this done and over with, but as a clinician yourself, you know that healing takes time." Dr. Natalie added, "I'm positive we'll make good progress, because I know how hard you're willing to work, but you need to remember that it's okay to take the time to go through the healing process thoughtfully and thoroughly." Michelle nodded with both truth and fear in her eyes. "Sleep, Michelle, is a good thing in times like this, though I expect that you will not have a lot of peaceful nights." Michelle knew then that Dr. Natalie understood she wanted to start this race and sprint to the finish line, regardless of how many sleepless nights or emotionally frustrating moments she encountered.

Dr. Natalie again reminded Michelle that it was okay to take her time. She reassured her that no matter what she shared, it would not change her deep admiration of and respect for her. Dr. Natalie knew that Michelle cared about her opinion of her. She had made such known during their first encounter when Michelle was seeking to become a doctor herself. Michelle greatly admired Dr. Natalie both as an individual and as a competent psychologist. They sat in silence for a long time as Michelle endeavored to find the words to express what she yearned to explain, both experiences and emotions.

After what felt like an eternity, Michelle broke the silence. "I am tired of feeling alone. I am tired of never being needed or wanted or included. I want friends who consider me more than an advisor. I want to feel more connected to my children. I want . . ." Tears filled her eyes, and as if on autopilot, Michelle pushed her emotions back. The boxes were still locked.

"You want what?" Dr. Natalie asked.

"Nothing. It doesn't matter."

"I think it does, Michelle. What do you want?"

Frustration returned as Michelle attempted to shut down the feeling of vulnerability. She wanted nothing, yet in truth she wanted for more than nothing. Michelle wanted love and acceptance for her adult self and the little child she was hiding. Michelle needed to get out of Dr. Natalie's office. She needed to get back into her safety zone. It was time that this session came to a close. "How about we talk about it next time?" Dr. Natalie didn't respond to Michelle's request. She knew that, given time, Michelle would say what needed to be said.

As the feeling of trust grew in the room, closed boxes began to crack. What did Michelle desire? With tears spilling down her face, Michelle declared what she had only shared in the private chamber of her heart. "I want to feel loved. I know that I am loved, and I know that the love others feel for me is genuine, but I just can't feel it. I want to. It is in some way all I have ever wanted." With waterfalls of emotions pushing forward, Michelle continued. "There are many in my life who express words of affection, and each time they do I smile, say thank you or note I love you too, yet there is this hollow feeling that stands in my heart. It's almost as if my head knows the words to the song but my heart can't find the beat. To my heart the words 'I love you' are just words, and I long for them to be so much more. I want them to be so much more, but I am not sure even how to make that happen. I am not sure how to allow myself to feel love."

"Thank you for trusting me enough to take the risk of sharing that. I know it wasn't easy for you, and I want you to know I understand the risk you have taken and that in my office, with me it is safe to make such confessions. I am here, and together we can work through this. You also need to know that this doesn't change the respect and admiration I feel towards you. You are safe here"

Michelle followed her open confession with a question: "How do I expose my heart so that I might feel love?"

"I think you know the answer to that. We open boxes, investigate and talk about the contents, empty the boxes, and then decide what to do with them."

Michelle knew that's what they needed to do. The true question was whether she had the courage to do it.

Michelle was willing to try, so her next question regarded which box they should begin with. There were so many—separate yet connected. "Thank you again, Dr. Natalie, for joining me in this journey. I get that we need to open boxes. But which ones and which one first? There are so many and a few I will not open."

"Well, Michelle, I think I know you and know how your faith, mind, and heart works. You will know which box, and together we'll find the keys to open them. There may be some that we will never open. Time will tell, but I think you already know the answer to that statement. I'll see you next week, and again thank you for trusting me. I am here, and I'll be here for as long as it takes."

"It better only take a few weeks."

Dr. Natalie just smiled as Michelle exited her office. She knew Michelle would sprint the whole way but that the finish line was more likely a matter of months versus weeks, and that if it had been any other client than Michelle it would be several years.

CHAPTER 7

The First Box: My New Home

Most individuals don't understand that effective healing happens in and out of the therapy office. Vulnerability is foundational in the remodeling process. Far too often, those who seek mending are unwilling or unable to reach the depths of vulnerable truth.

MICHELLE SPENT A FEW SLEEPLESS NIGHTS PONDERING DR. NATALIE'S remarks about opening boxes. Was it time? Could she really do this? How committed was she? What if she couldn't unearth her emotions? Could she share just a few of the boxes? "Gosh," Michelle thought, "at times I hate this therapeutic process. I know it works, but it only works if you are willing to do the work and I know what doing the work means." During their first round of therapy sessions in 1992, Dr. Natalie respectfully inquired about Michelle's neatly preserved, locked boxes. Michelle avoided her questions or answered with partial truths. Today, as she arrived for her session, she knew that the boxes she had avoided for so long would be placed in the office to be unlocked and emotionally examined.

As Michelle pondered what was about to begin, she contemplated which box to reveal first. She knew that each box would lead to another. Even though Michelle trusted Dr. Natalie, she knew there were some boxes that she did not want even Dr. Natalie to discover. Yet the clinical side of Michelle knew that if she wanted to heal completely, she could not unlock certain boxes while leaving others sealed. However, the client side of Michelle was hoping to find a way around opening all the boxes.

In this session, Michelle would unlock and open the box of childhood physical and emotional abuse. Discussing the content of this box would set the stage for further therapy discussions, discoveries, and healing.

Michelle started the session with the following thoughts: "I'm often astonished when my children recount details of their childhoods. Each of my children is able to share multiple memories enveloped in joy, laughter, and love. These memories range from Corduroy Bear bedtime stories to camping trips during which we hunted for dinosaur bones and warmed rocks in the fire to keep sleeping bags warm. My children recollect birthday parties and school activities and laughed about binge-watching *Sponge Bob Square Pants*. Each of my children has expressed appreciation that when they were growing up, our home was the place all their friends wanted to be. My children know without any reservation that they were always loved and always safe in our home."

In a halting voice Michelle disclosed, "I hold no such memories. I was born in the small town of Lititlz, Pennsylvania, to Russel and Julie Williams. Lititlz was also the birthplace of my Great-Aunt Vera Michelson, who was known as Auntie Vi. I was my father's third child and my mother's fourth. My parents later had two more children.

"I was due to enter the world on December 5, but my mom went into premature labor and gave birth on September 22, two and a half months early. I weighed less than two pounds, and according to a newspaper clipping that Auntie Vi later gave me, at the time of my birth I was the smallest baby born in the Lititlz Hospital to survive.

"My parents were not allowed to see me for the first few weeks of my life—the doctors thought it was best for my parents not to get attached since I would likely not survive. Perhaps the separation prevented my mom from bonding with me. Finally, after spending two months in the hospital, the doctors decided to send me home to be cared for by my parents because the hospital could provide no more medical assistance. I weighed just under four pounds, and the doctors were still concerned that I wouldn't make it. My parents kept me in a wooden box on top of a heater to keep me warm. When I cried, my mom would take me off the heater and place me in the car outside to avoid hearing my sounds.

"Auntie Vi told me that each time my mom put me in the car the next-door neighbor would call her to come get me. Auntie Vi said that in addition to being put in the car, I suffered from broken legs and severe burns—I still bear the burn scars—all before the age of five. I don't remember the broken bones or burns or whether my mother ever held me, helped me with my homework, or told me she loved me. If she did love me, did she care whether I was okay? Dr. Natalie, my childhood was void of feeling carefree. I don't think I ever laughed or smiled, let alone felt safe or loved. It's as though an inhumane eraser removed the typical childhood joy and replaced it with blackness that is incomprehensible. I must have been broken from day one. Maybe I still am." Michelle's voice trailed off into silence as her tears softly drummed Dr. Natalie's carpeted floor.

Michelle's childhood contained the type of horror that lurks in the crevices of the mind, invisible but ever present. Michelle thought unlocking the boxes would remind her why she thought she was bad, why she wasn't lovable, and why she deserved what had happened to her.

The box that Dr. Natalie and Michelle were unlocking in this session contained descriptions of what a child desperately wanted and what the child received instead. Michelle would be telling Dr. Natalie about the bad little girl she thought she was and had concealed for so long. It was time to bring forward the little girl Michelle hated, wanted nothing to do with, and had hoped and prayed would just go away. In Michelle's view, the younger her was dark, deformed, and weak. She was everything Michelle was not—at least, that's what she told herself.

"You know, Dr. Natalie, I would rather not talk about this. I would rather you didn't have to hear it, but we both know giving verbal voice to silenced memories ushers in healing. That is why we are here. It just cuts so deep"

"Yes, Michelle, I know that it does, but it's time you stop burdening all that darkness alone. I am here and you can take as long as you need."

After a long moment of silence Michelle began. "Dr. Natalie, on a cold winter day when I was around ten years old, I walked five miles home from school, as I did most days. I alternated between walking and running, hoping to get to the house before Mom so I could make sure all my chores, which I had completed that morning, were done according to her demands. I prayed that this time, Mom would be pleased with my hard work. I prayed that instead of being beaten, I'd receive a 'thank you.'

"As I entered the front yard and stepped up onto the porch, my mother opened the door and stepped outside. My father followed behind her. I froze. Mom had arrived home before me. Before I could say I was sorry, my mother informed my father and me that this 'thing'—referring to me—was no longer allowed in her home.

"I stood in silence, not sure what to say, just looking at her and then at my father. With no further words spoken, Mom went inside the house and locked the door, leaving me paralyzed. In the past, when I had failed in my chores, Mom would escort me to the location where I had performed unsatisfactorily and would ask questions such as, 'Why are you so stupid? Why can't you get it right? What is wrong with you?' To each question, I responded with 'I don't know.'" With tears in her eyes Michelle looked and Dr. Natalie and pleaded, "How is a child supposed to respond to that question? I didn't know why I was so stupid. I didn't' know why I couldn't get it right. Trust me, I spent most of my childhood asking myself that. My lack of satisfactory explanation to Julie's—I mean my mom's—questions infuriated her, and she would let out her fury physically, first with her hands and then with Dad's belt. If I resisted in any way, the whipping intensified. With each strike, I struggled to hold back tears as I silently asked myself over and over again why I was so stupid and couldn't get things right. She'd then leave me alone, bruised, and bleeding.

"Almost daily, I'd come home from school and find all the dishes removed from the cabinets with the instruction that I was to rewash them until I could learn to wash them correctly. At ten years old, dishwashing was a skill I clearly lacked competency in. I don't remember Mom ever teaching me the art of dishwashing. Her method of dishwashing instruction involved berating and beating me. During many of these beatings, Mom seemed to disassociate from me. With no warning, the blows would stop, and Mom would walk off, never offering any words of comfort or justification.

"I had expected similar retribution on the day that Mom and Dad met me on the porch. I must have done something particularly horrible because she gave me an even harsher punishment: I was to never enter our home again." Michelle's voice went silent for a few moments and then she noted, "You know, Dr. Natalie, my parents owned—and today my Dad still owns—a beautiful restored Victorian mansion. I love that house. I loved it as a small child. Although we know walls cannot talk, I know that house would have a lot to say. Odd. Guess you don't need to know that." Michelle again went silent as she sought to find the words and courage.

With a slight glisten in her eyes Michelle continued. "I didn't know what to do. I stood there for a long time. I felt numb, as if my entire emotional world had just been silenced. My young mind struggled to comprehend all the ramifications of my mother's most recent form of punishment. Where would I sleep, how would I eat, what about the bathroom? Surely Mom was not serious. Yet the door stayed closed. Not wanting neighbors to see and realize how bad I was, I moved to the back steps. As I sat there motionless in numbness, I reviewed my morning chores and prayed I could identify my failure so I could somehow fix it. No answers came.

"After what felt like forever, my dad found me on the back steps and informed me that he would provide his old work trailer as my new living space. I wanted to ask my dad a lot of questions, but I knew he had to do what Mom said." With deep sadness Michelle noted, "Dad always did what Mom wanted or she treated him like dirt. I felt so sorry for my dad growing up. I hated how my mom treated him. She was so unkind to him, and he was such a good man. That night as I moved my clothes into the old trailer, I pragmatically accepted that what was happening was just one more step in the life of a bad child. More proof that something was wrong with me. I can't even begin to explain the emptiness I felt. Looking back I think I was in shock, but then my young mind and heart were incapable of processing a mother's total rejection. I went from being a daughter to merely a thing. I just kept telling myself over and over, 'Fix it, Michelle, just fix it. What did you do wrong? Why are you so broken? Just fix it and you can go back into the house.' Something broke inside me that day, Dr. Natalie. I'm not sure what, but something. Looking back after all these years, I am not exactly sure how to explain how I felt. I am sure my mom had her reasons, but it felt cruel regardless of how bad I was."

Dr. Natalie just listened to Michelle while inviting her to continue. She knew Michelle needed to give audible voice to the content of the box they were now rummaging through.

"The next morning before school, Mom informed me that although I would no longer live in the home, I was still expected to get my chores done. She told me late enough that I had to choose between riding the bus to school or completing my chores. I didn't really have a choice, so I hurried inside and started my tasks. In the middle of washing the dishes, I realized that Mom was standing behind me. Dad had left that morning for the construction site he was working at. I turned to face Mom. She said nothing, but I won't ever forget the look in her eyes. Then she pinned me against the cabinets and started hitting me. I began to cry and pleaded with her to stop. Instead of stopping, in a fit of rage she aimed my dad's belt at my face and other parts of my head as she continued hitting me. Each time I moved my arms to protect myself, she shouted at me to lower them. I came to myself later, curled up in a ball on the kitchen floor, with Mom nowhere around. I must have blacked out.

"Slowly I attempted to stand so I could leave the house, but standing was impossible. Instead, I crawled back to the trailer. Back in the safety of my new home, I looked in the mirror. Both my eyes were blood red, with shades of purple discoloration around them and on other parts of my face."

Tears spilled down Michelle's face, and her voice cracked as she said, "I was so scared, Dr. Natalie. I had never seen red eyes before. I had no idea if I would be okay. I sat paralyzed by fear, wanting to know I would be okay but scared to ask—or for anyone to know what I had done. My ten-year-old mind wondered whether my eyes would ever be white again. I looked like a monster."

Dr. Natalie continued her silence, knowing Michelle needed to empty all the contents before they processed them. With flowing tears, bent shoulders, and eyes focused on the ground Michelle continued.

"What hurt far worse than the beating, the broken bones, the red eyes, or Mom's constant silence about my successes was everyone's' silence about my well-being. No one ever asked if I was okay. No one ever came to the trailer to check on me. Mom never told me she was sorry. Mom never said, 'I love you.' Mom never acknowledged that I was even human. To Mom, I was the whipping post she could take out her rage on at any time. Silence sealed the boxes of my abuse. Bones healed, eyes returned to white, and skin returned to its normal color, but silence remained both mine and theirs." Raising her head to meet Dr. Natalie's gaze Michelle concluded, "To this day, silence is tricky for me to process. I'd prefer that a person yell at me rather than ignore me.

"You might find this hard to believe, Dr. Natalie, but we never celebrated my birthdays, and on Christmas mornings, starting when I was around age ten, my mom made me come inside the home to watch my brothers and sisters open their presents while she'd tell me I wasn't given any gifts because I was a bad child. I tried so hard not to cry those Christmas mornings, praying to God that I could just get back to my trailer, where I could let out my emotions.

"I spent so many nights in tears as a child that when I got older, I vowed I'd never cry again. Well, today, as you can see, I'm not keeping that promise. This is stupid. Why does what happened matter? It was almost thirty-nine years ago."

Dr. Natalie nodded, accepting Michelle's frustration and knowing that their session, which had gone well past its allotted time, was allowing a box to empty.

"Can you imagine," Michelle said, "how it felt as a little child to know you were the only bad kid in the family? Why would a parent pick just one child?" Michelle asked in a pleading voice, seeking answers while still holding to the belief there must have been something wrong with her. Here in Dr. Natalie's office Michelle was not the trained psychologist Dr. Michelle Chambers. No, she was an isolated woman seeking to heal, and Dr. Natalie was ever mindful of that.

"You know, Michelle, it's not uncommon in dysfunctional families for one child to be singled out."

Yeah right, Michelle thought. *I was singled out because I was broken.* Michelle returned to verbally emptying the box.

"Shortly after I was banished to the trailer, kids at school made fun of me. They said I smelled funny. I remember one day when I was in gym class a student standing next to me started complaining about a horrible smell. He said it smelled like dirty socks. I just stood there paralyzed, knowing it was my socks. At that moment all I wanted to do was disappear. I guess that's why I wear perfume daily and make sure even when backpacking there are shower options." Michelle's voice trailed off as tears returned. "One night after weeks of teasing, I had enough courage to ask my mom if I could shower in the house. There was no water in the trailer. There was really nothing in that trailer. Gosh, that was a horrible place to live in.

"My mom just laughed and told me to bathe in the creek. Have you ever tried to take a bath in a frozen stream in the middle of winter? I had to break the ice to wash. Soap doesn't lather well in water that cold, and icicles formed in my hair. But the ice-cold water was better than the teasing, not that it ever really stopped. After my creek bath, I sat in my trailer and wondered whether I'd freeze to death. The electric heater my father had given me had stopped working many days before, and I had never been so cold. That night, I sat in the corner next to my makeshift bed, with my only quilt wrapped around me, and prayed that I'd warm up and that someone would come check on me. I was so scared that I would die that night. I was cold. As usual, no one came.

"When Mom kicked me out of the house, she also stopped buying anything for me. I occasionally received hand-me-down clothes from friends, and Auntie Vi would buy me new clothes and personal hygiene items during her visits to our home and when I was allowed to sleep over at her house. The first pair of shoes Auntie Vi purchased for me were a pair of Converse—red and white. To this day, I love Converse tennis shoes. I wear them every chance I get. Auntie Vi loved me, and she considered me a good child. She read me stories like 'Little Red Riding Hood' and 'Goldilocks and the Three Bears.' She took me out to eat, and she let me sleep beside her at night." Michelle's words halted as tears started to flow freely, which led the way to gut-wrenching sobs. After several moments of tearful despair Michelle whispered, "When I was nineteen, Auntie Vi drowned in a freak accident. Sadly, I was present. The only person who had ever shown me love as a child was taken from me. At first, I felt numb, and then the numbness turned to anger as I vacillated between being mad at God and then at myself because I could not save her.

"I tried, I tried so hard to save her, but I couldn't. Once again, I failed and again proved I couldn't do anything right. When everyone would tell me I was worthless and a nothing, I would hold Auntie Vi's words in my mind and for brief moments in all that hell remembered that she told me I was great and that she loved me, and I couldn't even save her." Silence returned to the office as Michelle allowed her emotions' presence. As tears subsided, Michelle continued.

"Do you know that my aunt invited me to speak and to share a few thoughts at Auntie Vi's funeral and my mother told me that it was not fair for me to speak at her funeral as I had other siblings who deserved to participate instead? So, I even let Julie—I mean Mom—take that from me. What was wrong with me? Why did I let her take that from me? I know I am the only person Auntie Vi would have wanted to speak, and yet I did nothing. I just stood there. What was is so wrong with me? Why can't I stand up to my mother?"

Again, Michelle's voice cracked as tears encompassed the room as she allowed herself to mourn the passing of the only person who truly offered her love and comfort in her childhood. As the tears shallowed, Michelle noted, "How blessed I was to spend the last few days of Auntie Vi's life with her. God granted me that gift.

"When I returned from Auntie Vi's house, Mom would throw away all of Auntie Vi's gifts."

With deep sadness and an inner child longing to understand, Michelle asked Dr. Natalie, "How can a person hate a child that much? I could never hate my children. I could never do to them what my mother did to me. Was I really that bad?"

Michelle looked up and was surprised to see tears shimmering in Dr. Natalie's eyes. She sat quietly for a minute before she broke the silence. "Michelle, we both know that no child deserves to be abused. I lack words to express the sorrow I feel for the abuse you experienced and for the loss of your Auntie Vi. I am so sad that you had to experience such." Though Michelle heard Dr. Natalie's words of love and concern for little Michelle, it would be months and many sessions before she could internalize them.

Dr. Natalie felt for the little Michelle more profoundly than Michelle could. She was still mad at her younger self for not getting things right and for just going silent. Michelle wondered whether her life would have been different if she had talked back. Her older brothers had talked back many times, and their mom had never touched them. In Michelle's mom's eyes, her brothers could do no wrong, whereas she could do no right.

Michelle spoke again. "The physical and emotional abuse hurt little Michelle, Dr. Natalie. I can admit it, but . . ."

"But what?" asked Dr. Natalie.

"How do you process knowing that your mother never loved you? That's all I wanted. That's all I have ever wanted." Tears flowed freely as hurt and sorrow for the little Michelle filled the room.

"Thank you for sharing, Michelle. I know it's not easy to do. Little Michelle was a strong and amazing little girl."

"No, she was not, Dr. Natalie. She was weak. She should have learned to do things right." The box was closing as the adult Michelle, competent and self-made, closed off the emotions of little Michelle. Michelle had shared enough for one day.

"Michelle, before you close your box and lock it, I have just one question. What do you think provided little Michelle with the ability to survive and become the amazing woman you are today?" Her question invited Michelle to see the younger her in a kinder light.

"Dr. Natalie, I'm not sure how to explain this, but for as long as I can remember, even as a little child, I believed in God. I wasn't raised in a religious home, but no matter how dark the days were, I would talk to my Heavenly Father. I just knew He was always there. You might find this odd, but He was like my imaginary friend, only I knew He was real. In all the aloneness, I talked to Him. I spent nights in that dark, empty trailer talking to Him out loud. On more than one occasion, I asked Him to please take me home. He didn't. Now, I'm so glad He didn't, but back then death felt so much better than one more day alone in a run-down trailer. Oh, how I hated the silence."

"Thank you for taking the risk to share this with me. Now I understand why communication is so important to you. Little Michelle really was remarkable, and, in time, I hope you'll let her talk as well. I respect what you shared as an adult today, but I wonder if the little Michelle would talk about these events differently."

"I have no idea if the little Michelle would, but I have no idea how to let the little me talk."

"You will in time. I'll see you next week."

"Thank you, Dr. Natalie."

As Michelle walked out of Dr. Natalie's office that night, she felt physically lighter. She recognized that it was okay to share with Dr. Natalie a dark part of her life. Michelle knew Dr. Natalie had listened with love and compassion, casting no judgment. Dr. Natalie's understanding and acceptance reaffirmed that Dr. Natalie was indeed the right person to take this journey with Michelle.

After Michelle climbed into her car, she called her best friend, Ivan. She told him she was going to see Dr. Natalie and was fairly certain he was curious about how the session went. Ivan had known Michelle for over twenty-nine years, and he perceived that her decision to meet with a psychologist indicated she wanted healing. Seeking out the assistance of a psychologist was a big step because Michelle previously believed that she didn't need help from anyone, not even Ivan.

Tonight, Dr. Natalie and Michelle had scratched the surface of her experiences as a little girl and had enabled Michelle to feel safe and cared for, if only for a few moments.

As Michelle called Ivan, little did she know that for the next eighteen months he would be her sounding board as she expressed frustration with and acceptance of Dr. Natalie's therapy procedures. Michelle does not know how many hours Ivan spent listening to her repeatedly express frustration, but she does know that regardless of the repetition, Ivan listened to her, loved her, and reminded her to trust the process and to trust Dr. Natalie. On almost every call, he'd also tell Michelle that she shouldn't quit therapy.

The first night Ivan asked, "So how did it go?"

Michelle responded, "Well, I'm not so sure I liked it, and I think it's senseless, but it went okay."

"Why do you think it's senseless?"

"Because I'm talking about crap that happened thirty-nine years ago and because Dr. Natalie thinks I need to learn to love little Michelle and to see how amazing she was, but—trust me—little Michelle was the total opposite of amazing."

"You sound a little frustrated."

"Yeah, but I do feel lighter."

"Why lighter?"

"I shared with Dr. Natalie some information regarding my childhood."

"That's great. I knew you needed to. When are you going back to see her?"

"Oh, really, and how would you know Mr. all wise and knowing?"

"Oh, my friend, you may think you have everyone fooled, but you do not fool me. As a matter of fact, I think I know you better than you know yourself."

"Funny, Ivan, very funny."

"I also know when this is all done there will be a lot more time spent with Michelle and a lot less time with Dr. Chambers."

"I am not Dr. Chambers with you."

"You are more than you realize, but that's okay because I know the real you, and I love the real Michelle."

"Hmm, well, I guess time will tell if you really do or not."

"Yes, yes it will. When do you go back?"

"Next week. You know, Ivan, maybe I should just forget the whole stupid process. I have a great life. Now is not the time to do this."

"Michelle, I know you, and you know you need this. So just suck it up and do it."

"Okay, thanks for listening. Talk to you tomorrow."

Ivan was right, even though Michelle hated that he was. That night, as Michelle entered her home, greeted by her children, she felt something had shifted. There was lightness amongst them, seriousness had faded a little, and there was a deeper feeling of connection

"Maybe even with my kids I have been Dr. Chambers" Michelle thought.

Michelle then offered a silent prayer of gratitude for the session she and Dr. Natalie had completed. God, her son, and Dr. Natalie helped provide the courage Michelle sought so that dark memories could be brought into the light and allow Michelle to no longer shoulder the burden alone. Tonight, Michelle would sleep deeper than she had done in many years.

CHAPTER 8

The Second Box: You Wanted It

The process of confession—the telling of one's story—has great healing power. Through confessing, an individual no longer needs to suffer in isolation. Confession invites another human soul in and allows both individuals to be edified and changed. Confession is a foundational, healthy part of therapy, for in the process of telling, burdens are lightened, and truth and love enter in through the help of the healer.

TYPICALLY, DR. NATALIE AND MICHELLE SCHEDULED ONE SESSION PER WEEK. However, when they were analyzing complicated topics, they would sometimes meet two or even three times a week. When Michelle felt it was essential to meet more than once a week, she would call Ivan, her sounding board, and confide in him why she needed to see Dr. Natalie again. Michelle would then counter her dialogue by arguing it was wrong to ask for so much time from Dr. Natalie. Due to Michelle's childhood, it was almost impossible for her to ask for what she needed. Ivan would listen with love and then tell her to call Dr. Natalie. Feeling even deeper frustration, Michelle would then restate all the reasons she couldn't call her. In response, Ivan would say, "Just call her. I know you will."

Sure enough, after they would hang up, Michelle would call Dr. Natalie and Dr. Natalie would make time to see her. Dr. Natalie knew that if Michelle was asking to see her before their next scheduled appointment, then the reason was significant.

Such was the case one week that Michelle met with Dr. Natalie three times. Michelle was ready to open the second box. During two of the appointments for the week, they skimmed the surface of Michelle's experiences. In the third session—which lasted three hours—Michelle exposed why she hated the little her and why she thought the little her was dark and ugly.

As Michelle entered Dr. Natalie's office for that third appointment, she wore Ray-Ban sunglasses and chose to sit as far away from Dr. Natalie as possible. They started the session with light conversation, and as Michelle responded to Dr. Natalie's questions with limited information, Dr. Natalie rose from her chair and turned down the office lights. Michelle thought, "What a kind way to invite me to remove my sunglasses without speaking."

Michelle took off her sunglasses and stared at Dr. Natalie's bookshelf instead of looking at her. She was filled with shame. She wanted so desperately to run out, slam the door, and never return, but she also yearned to remain in Dr. Natalie's office and unlock the second box. Michelle prayed that Dr. Natalie would help her find the strength to start the process of prying the lid open.

"Michelle, I want to thank you for asking me to see you again this week. I know how hard it is for you to ask for anything, let alone more of my time, and I'm pleased you did. I recognize that our last few sessions haven't gone smoothly. You've left frustrated and unnerved. What would you like to talk about today?"

Michelle thought, "What did I want to divulge? Better yet, how could I find the words to tell Dr. Natalie what I needed to confess? We'd danced around this box for a few sessions. Today, I knew the box was in the room, but I didn't have the faintest idea about how to begin unlocking it."

Dr. Natalie waited for Michelle to speak. The longer the silence lasted, the more shame Michelle felt. Finally, to escape emotional suffocation, Michelle whispered, "A few weeks ago, when we talked about my grandfather, I told you that I didn't like him and that he was an evil man."

"Yes, I remember. Go on."

"I didn't tell you why."

"I knew you weren't ready."

"Today, Dr. Natalie, I need to tell you why. Today I need to answer truthfully a few questions you asked me more than twenty-two years ago. The questions you asked me are the reason I didn't return to therapy. I couldn't lie, but I also couldn't talk about it then."

"I understand, Michelle. Are you ready to talk about it now?"

"I hope so. Do you remember the question you asked me?"

"Yes, I do."

Michelle withdrew from her briefcase a document and read the following:

"Most children grow up afraid of monsters in the closet or under the bed, wondering if the monsters will come out at night. For me, the monsters of my childhood weren't make-believe. They didn't hide under the bed. Instead, they were real and walked around in broad daylight, planning for the moments when they could create horror in my life and destroy any possibility of normalcy.

"I felt trepidation toward some of the monsters, whereas others I feared. Some of the villains only wanted my body, whereas others tried to destroy my soul. Some seemed intrusive, others weaved threads of darkness into my dreams each time I found myself the object of their infectious and twisted games. At times, some of the monsters offered consideration in the process of violating me, whereas the most dangerous barbarians afforded no consideration but derived pleasure from darkness, savagery, terror, and humiliation.

"These latter monsters were the ones I feared—and still fear—the most. From them, I could not escape, and in their presence, hell was created. The kind of hell which creates terror and confusion while weaving nightmares which know no boundaries of time. At the same time that I felt terror, I also felt confusion. I could never escape from them, and being in their presence was like being in hell. In this purgatory, my grandfather was Satan, and my aunts, uncles, brothers, and others were demons. They would reaffirm that they'd do whatever they wanted to me because I was bad, and my behavior warranted their actions. Because I was bad, they turned sheds into prisons. My relatives became wardens who possessed not only physical power but also ropes, sexual toys, other objects, and other children, all of which they used to punish and betray their prisoners.

"The monsters did whatever they wanted. When I cried or pleaded for them to stop, the torment only intensified. It's almost as if they found pleasure in my tears and thrived on my fear. To them, I was no more than an object through which to satisfy their sexual and physical desires."

After Michelle finished reading, Dr. Natalie sat in silence for a long time, seeking to gain personal composure before speaking. "Wow. Michelle, I am so sorry. I can't even begin to imagine the horrible experiences you endured. I don't have words to express what I am thinking and feeling. A child should never have to experience the life you were forced to live. That was an intense account. So, the answer to my question of whether you were sexually abused as a child is yes. The reason you don't like your grandfather and other members of your family is because they were the perpetrators."

"Yes."

"Thank you for taking the time to write about your experience. It provides me with a glimpse of what else happened during your childhood and explains why you like locked boxes. Again, I'm so sorry for the hell you were forced to live. How do you feel about what you wrote?"

"Fine. Lots of people have hard stuff happen in their lives; you and I both know that. What's done is done. I left all that behind me. I just needed to answer your question." Michelle had opened the next box and exposed some of the content, but the box was still concealing items, and Michelle was backing away to avoid feeling the emotions of what she had just read.

Dr. Natalie understood this, and she also understood that Michelle needed to do more than write down and read some of her experiences. She needed to verbally express anger, hurt, and loss and so she asked, "Michelle, when was the first time you were sexually abused, and who was the abuser?" Dr. Natalie was inviting Michelle to empty more of the box's collection through the sharing of feelings.

Michelle remained silent for what seemed like an eternity. "Dr. Natalie, I don't know how to answer. It cuts so deep. I have never talked about this with anyone. I am not sure I can do this. There are so many emotions and memories intermingled that the conglomeration almost feels like one massive wave of evil and shame with no beginning or end."

"It's okay, Michelle. Take your time. I'm right here."

With anger in her voice Michelle noted, "I hate that little girl. I hate what she did. I don't want to talk about this."

"I know, but I think you need to."

Michelle sat silent for several minutes, allowing her anger to still and then quietly started, "When I was seven years old, my father decided to work for his father-in-law, Viktor, who owned Viktor's Construction. Viktor's sons and sons-in-law also worked for the company, and when Viktor received a new project, all the family members—my grandparents, uncles, aunts, cousins, parents, and siblings—would pack up and move temporarily to the job site. Between the ages of seven and eighteen, for months at a time, I lived in Pennsylvania, Alabama, Delaware, Florida, Mississippi, Tennessee, Louisiana, Texas, and West Virginia. This moving caravan provided a living for the family and nightmares for me.

"You know, Dr. Natalie, I'd rather not examine this. I'm not sure I can put into words what you're asking me to tell you. There's so much obscurity." Tears once again formed in Michelle's eyes, and with slight anger in her voice she remarked, "How about we say we talked about it and just leave it alone for now? I do not need these tears, and I am fairly certain the hell you just asked about has no place in this office or any office, for that matter. I know, Dr. Natalie, that you and I, in our careers, have both been privilege to the hearing of difficult lives, but what I lack words to disentangle and describe will top the list. I do not need to relive the hell you just asked about. Ask me something else and just leave this alone."

"Do you think that will help you accomplish what you're trying to achieve by coming to my office?"

"No, but talking about something else sure sounds a lot easier. I don't even know how to explain what happened. There are no words to describe it. It's impossible to believe, let alone interpret."

Dr. Natalie sat quietly, allowing Michelle time in the process of disclosure.

"Okay, here goes. I think you'd describe what happened to me as generational incestuous abuse. Different members of my family would take turns forcing the younger kids to perform various sexual acts. My grandfather"—the anger in Michelle's voice returned and increased—"would pin me down between his legs with his knees by my shoulders and force me to . . . I'm sure you get the picture."

"Yes, I do. So, let's talk about how often the sexual abuse happened."

"It happened so often . . . It seemed like an everyday occurrence. God, I could never get away from it. When I think about it now it makes me sick. Reminds me how disgusting I was as a child. Do you have any idea what it is like to live knowing every day that those who are supposed to love you and protect you consider you only a toy to use for their sexual perversion? I hated it." Michelle's voice grew in anger. "I hated it." Michelle's voice increased volume and frustration. "Do you hear me? I hated it! At times I fought back, and at other times I just gave in. What the hell was wrong with me? It did not matter if I struggled. The results were the same. There were even times . . ." Again, Michelle's voice trailed off as anger gave way to gut-wrenching sobs. As the tears abated Michelle whispered, "Dr. Natalie, this hurts. I had no idea it was going to be this hard. I do not know if I can do this. I can't say it. I just can't. Let's just stop here. Please let's just stop."

"Yes, you can do this, Michelle. You are stronger than you think. There were times when what, Michelle?"

Still speaking softly, Michelle explained, "I really don't like that little girl. She was weak, and she should have fought every time. Instead, at times, she willingly participated." Tears were flowing freely down Michelle's face, and she made no attempt to hinder them. For several moments Michelle and Dr. Natalie sat in silence as tears flowed. Then in an almost unabideable voice Michelle continued, "Dr. Natalie, these encounters were the only times I was touched. The only times I was included. The only times I wasn't alone in the trailer. I just wanted to be loved. Why did I give in? What was wrong with me?

Now you know how ugly I am and why this conversation is over." Michelle shifted in her seat as her voice, fluctuating between hurt and anger, silenced.

"No, Michelle, I don't see ugliness. I see an amazing little girl who did what she had to do to survive so you could be who you are today."

"Yeah, right! The abuse during my childhood schooled me to be physically present but emotionally absent. I learned to shut down. When kids made fun of me, no tears were shed. When abusers requested services, I allowed my mind and heart to leave the room so that no emotions were tied to the sexual acts performed. I am not sure if I disassociated, but I know I chose to be numb. I compartmentalized emotions into boxes so that I survived. If I hadn't, all the stuff, all the humiliation I experienced on a daily basis would have literally killed me."

Seeking to shift Dr. Natalie's probing, or so Michelle thought, she added, "The thing that I hated the most about my two older brothers is that they would hold me down, for what felt like hours, just like my grandfather did. I would cry and plead for them to get off me, and my mom would just sit there and laugh. She thought it was funny. To this day, I don't do well if anyone tries to restrain me. If anyone wraps their arms around me in a playful way and tries to stop me from moving, I quickly escape or make it very clear I do not find such actions funny. At other times I just freeze, paralyzed, unable to move. My mom just laughed. Dr. Natalie, she just laughed. How is that possible? How can you laugh at a child who is being hurt? Because of what my older brothers did, I really don't like them. I've had very limited interaction with them in my adult life."

"So, we've moved from your grandfather to your older brothers. Why? Michelle, did they sexually abuse you?"

Michelle's voice caught in her throat. She needed air, she needed an escape. How did Dr. Natalie narrow in so quickly, and how could Michelle get away? Michelle stood with her arms folded and walked to the farthest corner in Dr. Natalie's office. Dr. Natalie went silent and waited for Michelle to respond. For a long time, Michelle just stood in the corner, secretly praying that a hole would appear and swallow her up. Yet no such hole materialized, and so Michelle stood for a long time just looking at the floor. She knew she needed to answer but that it would just lead to more questions. Ones she was not sure she was ready or strong enough to answer.

Silently Michelle slid to the floor and with lowered head and slumped shoulders whispered, "Yes, Dr. Natalie, they did."

"And how about your mom?"

The box's lid slammed shut. Deadbolts forced into place. Michelle stood, grabbed her briefcase, and headed for the door. This session was over. "Dr.

Natalie, I think we've talked through enough for one session. I'm done with this box. I'm leaving."

As Michelle turned the door handle and opened the door, Dr. Natalie wisely said, "Michelle, I know how much you want to leave, but would you please just sit back down for a moment? I have an assignment I'd like you to consider."

Out of respect for Dr. Natalie, Michelle closed the door. "What's my assignment?" Michelle asked in a rather curt voice. She wanted this session to end.

"First of all, thank you for trusting me. I know it was really hard to share what you told me today. Second, I'd like you to write a letter to that amazing little you."

"Amazing little me, are you kidding me? Did you not just hear what I told you she did? She let them do stuff to her. She didn't resist," Michelle verbalized with angry tones.

"Yes, I know, but I also heard you when you said it was the only time you were touched and included. What would you tell a client if they told you what you just told me?"

"That's not a fair question. You can't play that card."

"Oh, I think it is, and yes I can. Dr. Chambers, what would you tell them?"

Tears of freedom pulled forward and replaced Michelle's pride. She returned to the couch and cried for a long time, allowing the second box to almost empty. As the tears slowed, Michelle stated, "I would tell my client how strong they were and that they did what they had to in order to survive." Michelle admitted that as she said those words, she also thought, "But I'm the exception to the rule. I knew better. I knew it was wrong, and I still did it." There would be many more sessions and art therapy projects completed before Michelle could learn to love and accept the little Michelle. For now, she was receptive to Dr. Natalie's homework assignment.

As Michelle drove out of the parking lot that night, after waiting for Dr. Natalie to finish paperwork and safely leave her office, she knew something inside of her was starting to shift. Indeed, truth was setting both her and her little Michelle free. This session had been difficult. Yet, in that difficulty, darkness was exposed to light, and love was replacing shame. Michelle had told Dr. Natalie a few of her darkest secrets, and instead of casting blame, Dr. Natalie expressed love and understanding while inviting Michelle to change her vision.

Tears again flowed in the quiet of Michelle's car, but this time the tears weren't from anguish but from hope. She no longer had to carry her burden alone, and it was okay that another person knew about the terrible little girl she had been concealing. Michelle said a prayer of thanksgiving for Dr. Natalie's compassion, expertise, love, and non-judgement. For now, anyway, Michelle thought. After all, Dr. Natalie didn't know the whole story yet. Michelle also thanked Heavenly Father for standing beside her during this difficult journey, just as He had thus far in her life. Michelle truly had not been, nor would be, alone in this spiritual healing journey.

As the tears abated for a moment, Michelle called Ivan, ready to share with her best friend her expressions of gratitude and if she felt so prompted to tell one more person about some of the abuse she experienced as a child.

Ivan answered on the third ring. "So how did it go?"

"It was hard. Harder than I ever thought it would be, but I think worth it, although the jury is still out on that one."

"Yeah, why was it so hard?"

"Dr. Natalie and I opened an other box regarding some events in my childhood that were hard to talk about. Well, we didn't really talk about them. It was more like I admitted to them. I am sure in our next sessions to come we will have further discussion about them. Trust me, I doubt Dr. Natalie will let me get off easy regarding this box.

"All I could do tonight was admit something happened. That admitting was a very difficult emotional process."

"Why, did Dr. Natalie get to see the strong iron Michelle cry?"

"You're too funny, Ivan, too funny."

"I know I am, but more important than that, did you let her in? Did you share your feelings with her?"

"Yes, Ivan, I did."

"That's great! That is true strength. You are so strong. I'm so happy for you."

"Really, I think your happiness is rather sadistic. I tell you that I cried, and you're happy?"

"Oh, yes. You needed to cry, and you need to cry a lot, and I know you trust Dr. Natalie so you will let her see your tears and that is so healing. I don't know what happened to you, and it's okay if you don't want tell me. I'm just so happy you are finally healing."

The phone went silent for a long time, and then through more tears Michelle said, "Ivan when I was a child, I was sexually abused by different members of my family, and tonight Dr. Natalie and I began the process of talking about a few of those events."

"I am so sorry that happened to you, my friend. I want you to know I love you and think you are strong and amazing. I am so happy you've decided to heal. Thank you for trusting me enough to tell me, and know I am here for you no matter how long it takes or what you need."

"Thank you, Ivan. We've been friends for a long time, which has been such a blessing in my life."

"Yes, and we will be friends until we are old and senile, and then we will be new friends all over again."

"Oh, Ivan, you always know how to make me laugh. Thank you."

"When do you see Dr. Natalie again?"

"Next week."

"Okay, go home and get some sleep. Oh, and by the way, if more tears come, please let them come. And if you need to talk to someone in the middle of the night, like at 3 a.m., call Dr. Natalie. Just kidding, call me. Okay, love you, my friend."

"Good night."

As Michelle and Ivan finished their phone call, tears mingled with anger filled Michelle's Cadillac as her drive home included an endless parade of memories across her mental stage. In full view, with no more obscurity, Michelle saw the little her full of self-hatred as well as strength. The little her seated in the corner of her trailer, the little girl being led by her grandfather's hand, the little girl seated in front of a broken heater, the little girl picked last for school teams, the little girl, yes, the little girl pleading for forgiveness, love, warmth, kindness, and acceptance.

"God, please stop these memories. It hurts too deep. I can't do this. Please take it from me. All my life I have run from them and successfully so. Boxes have served their purpose granting me the ability to live the life I wanted and to become the person you needed me to be. I am nothing like those who raised me. Why must I go back in order to heal? Why, God? Just make it stop! I can't do this. Please, God, there is so much pain, there is so much darkness." Michelle's voice of anger broke, giving way to mournful tears. "That little girl is so broken and wrong. Please give me the strength to silence her, but no, no you don't want her silenced, do you? You want her to have a voice. How I hate this therapeutic process. How in the world do I write a letter to a person I want nothing to do with?"

Michelle pulled over, allowing her Cadillac to shift from an encased tomb of despair to a private surrendering embrace with her Heavenly Father.

Later that week, once Michelle was able to relock the box she and Dr. Natalie had opened, she drafted the required letter. The executive Michelle sharing her perspectives of the condemned little Michelle.

"Hmm, that was not as hard as I thought it was going to be, but then sharing it might be a whole different story," thought Michelle. "I guess time will tell. Now to get back to my work on my desk and put all this therapy stuff aside." Easier said than done.

CHAPTER 9

The Third Box:
The Invisible Child

Many therapists limit the treatment process by considering the relationship with the client to be insignificant. It isn't. Beautiful gifts are possible if the client feels safe discussing his or her emotions with the therapist and if the therapist understands the sacredness of the therapist–client relationship.

AT MICHELLE'S NEXT SESSION, SHE SELECTED A SEAT CLOSER TO DR. Natalie. Michelle figured that this appointment would be lighter and that no extra space would be necessary. She was wrong. Most sessions with Dr. Natalie were weighty.

"How are you, Michelle? I know our last session was pretty tough."

"Yes, it was. I cried most of the way home, and my tears went throughout the night and opened the flood gates of sadness as well as anger. At moments I was able to identify the reasons for my tears and anger, but most of the time my heart just felt this overwhelming need to mourn for the loss of innocence. When the tears finally abated and anger stopped, I felt lighter and some peace, but that night was not easy, Dr. Natalie. I think at moments I thought I was going to die, it just hurt so deeply. It has been a long time since I cried that hard and for that long. I think the last time I cried like that was when I was a child and I told myself then I would never ever cry like that again. Well, as you can see, I broke that promise. Seems that due to this therapy process I am breaking quite a few promises I made to myself as a child."

"I'm sure that was really hard, but that is so good. Thank you for telling me. I continue to be impressed by how intense the therapeutic process is for you. Many clients avoid such depths. It's a gift to work with a client who's willing to do the hard work of emotional healing. Thank you again for allowing me to be part of your journey. Where would you like to start today?"

As Michelle listened to Dr. Natalie's words, she wondered whether Dr. Natalie truly understood how impactful her guiding role was in her healing. Their relationship of trust provided the foundation for growth and renewal. Dr. Natalie and Michelle had discussed that they knew that God had brought the two of them together so that they could both know the crucibles of healing. Being seated in Dr. Natalie's office was no mere coincidence, and they both, as clinical experts and as doctor and patient, understood the sacredness of their connection.

Michelle opened her briefcase and pulled out her completed homework assignment. Then she began to read it out loud.

Dear Michelle,

"When the adult me thinks about you, I pretend that you don't exist. If you force me to acknowledge your presence, then I'll conclude that everything you went through was just a nightmare that will end by waking up.

When the adult me pauses to think of you, I'm judgmental. I deny your existence. I hope that if I reject you long enough, then you'll leave me alone. I run from you, and most of the time I'm very successful, but there are junctures when you catch me. In those moments, I feel lost and overwhelmed with emotions begging to be acknowledged and explored. Instead of granting your presence, I dig deeper to conceal you. I add more to my schedule and sprint on, praying you'll be left behind. In truth, I fear that someday I'll no longer be able to hide you. When that time comes, you'll shatter my false reality and force me to see how defective I am.

I've silenced your voice and forced you into a corner. I denied your emotions, minimized your pain, and viewed you as weak. I blamed you, not my perpetrators. In my eyes, you were used and broken. I hate the fact that you had feelings, that you gave in. The most damaging knowledge to my adult self is the fact that, at moments, you needed what your perpetrators offered. How could you? How could you ever hunger for their filth? Seeking for those touches made you like them. What happened to you was your fault. If you had only kept fighting, then I wouldn't have to run away from you. I live in fear that your shameful actions will be discovered and destroy the adult me. Then, once again thanks to you, I'll find myself alone, unwanted, abused, and silent.

Now, as I look at you during this healing experiment, I realize that I've treated you the same as your wardens and fellow inmates did. I've denied you the right to be seen and to be heard. I have not allowed you to feel, or to be accepted. I have taken away your right to dream and to hope. I have made certain you are not allowed to cry or to trust. Most significantly, I have denied you the right to be loved. Just as your abusers did, I've silenced the little girl. I've expected you to be still, to tell no one that you existed, while I've been living in two worlds: the world in which everyone sees the adult me as reliable and competent, and the silent world in which I experienced an abusive childhood. Both of these worlds put us behind the bars of denial, allowing us to almost exist but never letting us live freely in either place.

With respect,
Michelle

After finishing, Michelle handed the letter to Dr. Natalie. She reviewed it for a few moments and then asked, "How do you feel about the letter?"

"Fine. I thought it was going to be hard to write, but it wasn't that bad."

Dr. Natalie nodded and then said, "This is really well written, and I know it is heartfelt, but I'm struck by its lack of emotion and feeling. It seems more like a letter written to an adult than a child . . . I'm also struck by the fact that many of these messages to your younger self are full of blame, not empathy. Last week you allowed yourself to cry for the little you, but your letter has no tears."

Ouch! Michelle could see her point, but she was still fighting the internal battle of self-hatred and denial. Michelle was unsure how to shift from self-blame to self-acceptance. The little Michelle had done horrific things. Michelle couldn't forgive her. She didn't want to get to know her. Michelle wrote the letter—that was good enough.

"Dr. Natalie, first of all, I did what you asked. She deserves the letter I wrote. You do not know the whole story, and I am sure once you do you will agree. I'm not sure how to change my feelings toward the little me. There's so much darkness. I've spent so many years locking her away."

"I can understand that, Michelle. Part of the reason you can't find the key to set her free is that you judge her based on your current knowledge and situation. When we talk about the abuse that little Michelle experienced, you acknowledge she was a child, but you view those abusive events through the eyes of a forty-nine-year-old, not the eyes of a ten-year-old just praying to make it through one more night. I'd like you to write another letter to little Michelle. This time, as you write your thoughts, I need you to picture a little girl, lost, alone, and broken. Can you do that?"

"Are you kidding? I told you when we started this journey, I was only going to give it a few weeks. It has already been a few weeks and I am getting ready to be done. I wrote the letter, didn't I? I have no desire to do a rewrite."

"Okay, let me ask you this. How many times did you have to do a rewrite on your dissertation?"

"What does my dissertation have to do with this?"

"Just humor me and answer the question."

"More times than I can count."

"Why did you do the rewrites?"

"It was important to get it right; it mattered a lot, at least it did to me."

"What about the journey we are on now—how much does it matter to you? Is this your life dissertation? You told me at the start of our work together that this time you would complete the journey, and you knew it would require vulnerability as well as strength. That's what I'm asking for now. I know you and I know you always keep your promises. You need to do this."

"You know, Dr. Natalie, I am starting to really hate this process. I just want to be done."

"I know, Michelle. I know, and we will get there, I promise."

"I can try, but I am not sure how to write a different letter, and I'm not sure it will work, but I will try."

"Part of your healing journey will include coming to accept and love your younger self. If you can't learn to embrace her, then your progression will be limited. I love little Michelle. When I visualize her, I see this determined little girl who stood up against Goliaths even when she knew they would knock her down. They hurt Michelle, but they didn't destroy her. She's the reason you're here."

"Yes, I know that, Dr. Natalie!"

"No, I don't mean that she's the reason you're in my office; she's the reason you're on this planet, still alive, still making a difference in the world, and raising four amazing children."

"Sure. You say you love her and think she's resilient." Anger filled Michelle, and each of her words became sharper. "You don't know her the way I know her."

Dr. Natalie remained silent, allowing stillness to return to the room so that anger could be replaced with compassion and understanding.

"Do you want to talk about it, Michelle?"

"Talk about what?"

"Before our last session ended, I asked you a question."

Michelle nodded and felt the blood drain from my face.

"You didn't answer the question. Are you ready to talk about it now?"

"No. It's not possible. There's no way a mother could ever sexually abuse her child. It's unimaginable. The answer to your question is no. No. You and I both know clinically," Michelle said in a pointed voice, "such is highly unlikely, and if such does happen the damage can be catastrophic. My life is not in shambles. I am a very confident and successful individual. No, the answer is no, and do not ever ask me that again. *No!* Is that clear?"

"Okay." Dr. Natalie wisely set the topic aside, knowing that Michelle's anger was answer enough. "We're getting close to the end of this session. As I mentioned before, I'd like you to write another letter to little Michelle, but this time I want you to try to see her, not talk through her."

"Sure, okay. See you next week." Michelle agreed not because she wanted to do it but because she wanted out of Dr. Natalie Stachowski's office.

As Michelle left Dr. Natalie's office, instead of feeling release and peace, she felt angry. Frustrated. Afraid. How was she supposed to write a different type of letter? Michelle couldn't go back and be that little girl. She was done with little Michelle. Little Michelle belonged in the past. When Michelle had started this round of therapy, spending time with little Michelle was not on her agenda. Little Michelle just needed to go away. "God," Michelle verbalized in the privacy of her car, "what do I do now? I can't do this. I promised to heal, to be vulnerable, to be raw, but this . . . this is asking too much. You know I can't do this, and you know I won't do this. But I promised Dr. Natalie. I promised. I am just going to quit. That's it! I'm done! I'm not coming back."

Michelle put her Cadillac in gear and burned rubber out of the parking lot. She needed to get as far away from Dr. Natalie's office as possible. "Maybe now is a good time to take up drinking," thought Michelle. This time chai tea would not help, but perhaps fast miles on her car would. Michelle knew her Cadillac could almost fly.

After about a hundred and fifty miles were behind her, Michelle's desire to escape calmed and she called Ivan. Without even waiting for a hello, Michelle exploded. "Ivan, this whole process is idiotic, and I'm not going back. I thought I needed to start this round of therapy, but tonight I'm positive I was wrong. I'm done!"

Ivan patiently listened to Michelle and then asked, "What happened with Dr. Natalie that's made you so furious?"

Michelle told him about the letter she had written and that Dr. Natalie wanted her to try again.

"So, you're this mad over a few letters? That's slightly overreactive. Did anything else happen during your session?"

Michelle froze, unsure of how to respond. Yes, something else had happened in Dr. Natalie's office, and it had everything to do with Michelle's anger, but she did not want to discuss this topic with Ivan. She and Ivan had always been open with each other, but tonight Ivan had asked Michelle a question she did not want to answer.

"Ivan, I need to make a call. I'll call you back." Michelle quickly hung up. Usually, Ivan gave her perspective and reminded Michelle of why she needed therapy. Tonight, talking with him only increased her frustration. Now, Michelle was running from two people whom she loved and trusted deeply. Instead of heading home, Michelle turned her Cadillac toward the mountains. She needed more time, which driving and hiking provided.

The next morning, Michelle called Dr. Natalie's office and canceled their second appointment for that week, noting that she needed to go out of town. Michelle had texted an old friend during her drive and asked whether now was a good time to visit her in Louisville, Kentucky. Lucky for Michelle, she said yes. Michelle packed a bag, loaded her bike, and embarked on the twelve-hour drive. When Michelle canceled her appointment, Dr. Natalie called back and left a voice mail offering to meet via a phone call during her drive. Michelle wasn't sure she wanted to talk with Dr. Natalie. Michelle began her drive, and as the miles passed, a game of mental tug-of-war ensued in her mind.

One side pulled: you need to take Dr. Natalie's call. The other side heaved: no way; I'm done. Eventually, in both frustration and surrender, Michelle texted Dr. Natalie to tell her that she was open to a phone call if she had time. About an hour later, just when Michelle figured Dr. Natalie was occupied, a text arrived. Dr. Natalie was asking whether they could talk in about thirty minutes, during Dr. Natalie's drive home. Michelle was both relieved and shaken. If she was lucky, there would be no cell service when Dr. Natalie called. Michelle texted back and then started praying for the courage to say what they both knew she needed to say.

Michelle's phone rang. Again, the mental tug-of-war began. "Do I answer? Do I just let it go to voice mail? I can still get out of this." After four rings, she answered. As Dr. Natalie and Michelle engaged in small talk about her trip, Michelle's trepidation subsided. She could trust Dr. Natalie. Dr. Natalie cared. Toward the end of the conversation, with peace between them, Michelle confessed to Dr. Natalie, "When I get back, there's something I need to tell you."

"I know, Michelle, and it will be okay."

"I'm not sure how to tell you."

"I know that as well, and it will be okay. You will know when it's the right time to tell me. There's no pressure."

"Okay."

"Drive safe, and I'll see you when you get back."

Both stillness and emptiness returned to the vehicle. With each passing mile, Michelle tried to silence the voices in her head while discarding the rising feeling in her heart. She just wanted to enjoy a good weekend with her friend. "Please, God, just let me have peace this weekend. I need time. I just need time." Although Michelle enjoyed space away from therapy, the conversation constantly lurking in her mind was the rising reality that only complete rawness would break locks, empty boxes, and allow love to enter in. The night before Michelle headed for home seated next to a warm fire on a lake bed with her friend close by, Michelle drafted two letters.

During Michelle's trip, Dr. Natalie's receptionist called to schedule a time for her to meet with Dr. Natalie after she was back in town. Dr. Natalie wanted to see Michelle right away, so Michelle went to her office the evening after she returned. Michelle knew it was time to open the next box and to talk about the question Dr. Natalie had asked in their last session. Michelle realized deep within her heart that she had to keep moving forward, for if she stopped, she might never open the reaming boxes.

As Michelle entered Dr. Natalie's office, she wasn't sure where to sit. Because of the late hour, sunglasses weren't really an option, but Michelle still considered wearing them. With some hesitation, she decided that sitting at the end of the couch would be best, although she seriously considered sitting in Dr. Natalie's desk chair so that she might assume a more professional role.

"How are you, Michelle? How was your vacation?"

"I'm fine, and it was excellent. Thank you for asking."

"Where do you want to start tonight?"

Michelle sat still for a long time, pleading for both strength and understanding, and then started. "I have the letter you asked me to write. How about we start with that?"

"That would be a great place to start."

"Dear Michelle,

"I've contemplated writing this letter more times than I can count. Until recently, my writing attempts were full of animosity and disdain toward you. For many years I blamed you. Why didn't you get it right? Why weren't you strong? What was so wrong with you? Why did you respond physically when they touched you? Why did you stop fighting and let them do what they wanted? I viewed you as unclean and broken. For years, I ran from you, but no matter how far away I went, you showed up again. It was like a recurring nightmare. I lived in fear that others would see you. I could never get away from your stain.

"Now, as locks have opened, the truth has been revealed and I no longer see a broken individual. Rather, I see a little girl who was more resilient than I was willing to admit. I see a confused little girl hurt and pleading to be loved. A little girl who stood when so many would have caved. A little girl who took abuse without ever striking back and hurting others. A little girl forced into a corner, scared that the next whip of the belt might end her life. A little girl who could have chosen to stop living but didn't. A little girl who could have chosen to repeat the nightmare she lived in but didn't.

"You broke the chains of abuse, deciding to live a life filled with faith that was consecrated in striving to be perfect. You gave up trying to be loved, you turned off the ability to feel, and you chose to hold on, even if for only one more day. Now, instead of seeing you as damaged, I feel your hurt. I feel your sadness. I hear your pleadings, I know your fear, and, most importantly, your hope that someday you would be loved for who you were and not what for what you did. All you ever desired was to be loved.

"I am so sorry that instead of being loved and protected, you were violated. I'm sorry that many turned a blind eye to your suffering and made you feel invisible. I'm sorry that I couldn't protect you, that I couldn't stop the pain. I'm sorry you felt alone and scared.

"I can see you now, though it's difficult to do so and to accept the truth about the childhood you lived. I never wanted to recognize your childhood, nor did I want anyone else to ever know what happened to you. I kept you silent, and I hurt you by denying you the voice of truth. I pretended that what happened to you was no big deal. I hid from reality. I pretended that your childhood was typical. Oh, how sorry I am for what you went through. How I wish I could hold you and let you cry. How I wish I could wrap my arms around you and tell you over and over again that you are worth loving and that someday it's going to be okay. Eventually, the pain, fear, suffering, and sorrow you feel will end. Someday you'll leave this nightmare and never go back.

"Oh, Michelle, how did you ever survive what they did to you? How did you ever get out of there? How did you ever learn to be the person you are?

"With admiration,

"Older Michelle."

"Wow! This is a much different, and more caring letter; thank you. I can tell that you spent time allowing both the little Michelle and the older Michelle to do hard work. This letter is a good start. You allowed yourself to see the little you. How do you feel about this letter?"

"This letter was harder to write, Dr. Natalie, but it feels more authentic. I spent a bit of time in the woods on my trip arguing with you and God in my head and heart. Part of that argument was a pleading to allow me to see my younger self in a less judgmental light. The other part was a plea of escape. I just wanted out. My mental arguing allowed my younger self in full view before me as I emotionally worked to see some good in her instead of just the bad. My trip and the writing of this letter allowed me to process some of what little Michelle went through. In that processing I gained a small glimpse of her strength. I know I still have a long way to go before I completely accept her, but I'm getting closer."

"What do you feel is the biggest hurdle you have to overcome so that you can continue the process of accepting little Michelle?"

"I have a tough time picturing myself as a child. I've always felt like an old soul. I see life and events differently than most individuals do. I also know I hold myself to a higher standard than what I expect of others. An aunt once told me that the reason my mother hated me was because I was thirty years old when I was only five. It was an odd statement, but maybe it was true. Perhaps Julie felt intimated by her own daughter.

"You might find this of interest. When I was in second grade, I completed an IQ test. The test results placed me in the top tenth percentile in the nation. Supposedly I was brilliant, yet I was in special education at school. How's that possible? Because of my IQ score, I was tested every school year. Sadly, my mother often used my IQ results against me."

"How so?"

"If I had a low grade, she'd say I was lazy since school was presumably easy for me. In contrast, she'd emphasize how hard school was for my older brothers and how hard they had to work."

"You know, Michelle, I have a difficult time finding too much to like about Julie."

"Yeah, me too, but most people who meet Julie love her. They think she's so amazing. I believe that the Julie who raised me and the Julie whom everyone else knew and loved were two different people. I used to listen to her tell people what a horrible child I was. She had no shame."

Dr. Natalie let Michelle vent for a while, then asked, "Are you ready to unbolt the next box?"

Michelle felt paralyzed, wanting to heal but not to participate in the suggested conversation. Looking through tears Michelle pleaded, "I'm okay if we just close the session here."

With deep compassion Dr. Natalie replied, "Are you sure? During our phone conversation, you indicated there was something you needed to tell me."

"Yes, that's true, but the hour is almost up, and I know this conversation is going to take time."

"Michelle, we have time."

Dr. Natalie was in the habit of setting Michelle's appointment as her last session for the day; that way, they could take whatever time was needed—sometimes two hours. This accommodation was a special gift—a way of showing Michelle how much she cared and how vital their healing work was. Finally, after what seemed like an eternity, Michelle spoke.

"I decided to address this box by writing a letter from little Michelle's perspective. So far, writing has played a principal part in our work. Some of the events I wrote about are things we've already covered. There are, however, some new things to talk about that are in the box in the room tonight."

"That's good. Are you ready to share these things?"

"I'm not sure. Dr. Natalie, there are parts of my childhood I'd rather not talk about. Can we leave this box locked and still complete healing?"

"I think you know the answer to that question. What would you tell a client if he or she asked you the question that you just asked me?"

"Oh, that's not fair."

"I think it is."

Michelle returned to silence. Dr. Natalie was right. Michelle would tell her client exactly what Dr. Natalie had said to her. No matter how dark or painful a box's contents are, all the boxes have to be unlocked and emptied so that love can enter and heal.

"Dr. Natalie, I just can't do this."

"Yes, Michelle, you can, and I'll be right here. You can do this."

"This isn't going to be easy to hear, Dr. Natalie."

"Michelle, of course it's hard to hear what you need to say, but I know you need to bring those things into the light. I'm grateful that you trust me enough that you're willing to open up and empty this box with me."

"You're not going to like what I wrote."

"That's okay. I don't need to like it. I just need to hear it so that you can let little Michelle—and adult Michelle—heal. We both know the power of this type of work."

"How about you read what I wrote instead of having me read it? Then you'll know what needs to be explored and we can move to the next box." Dr. Natalie didn't say anything, but she nodded her head to acknowledge Michelle's reference to additional boxes.

"Okay, Dr. Natalie, I'll read it." In a halting voice through tears of complete shame and hurt, Michelle read the following:

ALONE

It's so cold. I have my blanket around me, but I can't get warm. I can see the lights on in the house. I wonder what you're doing. Do you even know that I'm cold? Do you even care if I am afraid? Do you even see me? I just want to be next to you. I hope to make you proud of me. I just want you to love me. Am I so broken that you can't love me? Why can't I get things right? Why do I make you so angry? Why can't you see that I'm trying so hard to do what you want so you can love me? You're playing games and laughing. Why can't I come in? You don't need to let me play. I can just watch. Did you ever love me? I feel so lost. I feel so sad. I feel so alone. Please, please just let me come inside. Please, can't you just love me? Mom, I'm hurting. Please help stop the pain.

INSIDE

I hear your car pull into the driveway, and I'm still in the house. I'm so scared it feels like I can't breathe. I work as fast as I can. I try so hard not to be in the house when you get home. When you come in, I think that today I'll get it right. Today, you'll love me. You'll be so proud of the work I've done. These thoughts make me freeze. I'm afraid to talk.

You talk to me, but I'm silent. You ask me why I'm so stupid and why I can't get anything right. I don't know what to say. Like you, I wonder why I'm so stupid and why I can't get anything right, but I don't know how to tell you that. You check my work. Each time you find a mistake, your anger rises.

I know what's coming. I back away. I try to hide, to become small. Maybe you won't see me. Perhaps I can get away. No, I never get away. You come at me. There's so much rage in your eyes. I tell you over and over again that I'm so sorry. I'm so sorry. I tried—I really did. You scream at me, telling me how bad I am. How stupid I am. That I didn't try. That if I had tried, the house would be clean. You begin hitting me. I try to put my hands up, but you scream even more and tell me to put my hands down. I lower them and try to turn to protect my face, but it's no use. You keep hitting me. You pause for a moment, and I think it is over. I think that

I made it, but no, you've only stopped so you can go get Dad's belt. The blows resume. I fall to the floor, but you don't stop. I want to ask you to stop, but I know that if I speak, you'll get madder. So I remain silent. You keep yelling at me: Why am I so stupid? Why can't I complete my chores correctly? What's wrong with me? I don't know, but I wish I did.

You step back and then walk away. I crawl to the door and head for my trailer. I hurt. I'm cold. I'm so sorry. I sit in the corner and cry. I'll get it right tomorrow. Then I wonder whether I'll live. I look in the mirror and see that my face is swelling and my eyes are red. I'm so scared. Please come hold me. Please check to see if I'm okay. I promise I won't be mad. I know it's my fault. I know I'm bad. Can you please just see if I am okay? Can you please love me? All I want you to do is to love me.

UNKNOWN

My brother is knocking on the door of my trailer. Why? What does he want? He says, 'You have to come inside. Mom wants you.'

No. I don't want to go inside. Dad isn't at home. It's too late to do chores. I don't want to go in, but I know I have to. It's a long walk into the house. Nathan is holding the door open to the house. He's smiling at me—in a way that says things are going to happen. He knows what you want. I want to run back to the trailer, but I know I can't. You are in the doorway of your bedroom, not wearing any clothes. I back away. I want to return to my trailer. You move toward me and pull me into your room. The door closes. You are in the bed beside me. Then you are on top of me. I close my eyes. I don't understand what you want. You are not screaming or angry. I don't want to . . . Can't you hold me instead? I'm scared. I'm confused. I don't move. The world goes dark.

I'm back in my trailer. It's cold. I hurt. I'm confused. I feel sick, strange, and alone. Tears fall. Nathan always sleeps with you when Dad's gone. Now I know why you never wear clothes in bed. I'm numb. I don't understand. Why can't anyone love me? Or is this love? What's so wrong with me? I talk to God. I know He hears me. I ask Him to take me home. I know He can, just for a little while. I sit in the corner, trying to get warm. It's so cold. I fall asleep."

After Michelle finished reading the condemning manuscript, she folded it in her hands. Michelle had just unlocked a box and spilled its hideous contents all over Dr. Natalie's office floor. She wanted to pick up the exposed scraps, stuff them back in the box, and run out of Dr. Natalie's office, never to return. Dr. Natalie now knew what Michelle had promised never to disclose. Now, Dr. Natalie knew why Michelle hated little Michelle. Dr. Natalie knew why the little and adult Michelle were so ugly and unworthy of love. She knew why

Michelle kept a barrier between her and everyone she knew: Michelle couldn't risk having those she loved and cared about discover this incomprehensible darkness. As these thoughts ran through Michelle's mind, tears started to fall, as if seeking to offer comfort to her emotional turmoil.

Dr. Natalie broke the silence. "Michelle, I'm so sorry. There are no words that can adequately express my deep sadness for you and my disdain for Julie." Tears filled Dr. Natalie's eyes. "She wasn't a mother to you. How you ever made it through your childhood is difficult to comprehend. You were an amazingly strong girl. What are you feeling?"

"What *was* I feeling? Shame? Yes, shame darker than what I've ever known. What *am* I feeling? Hatred. Hatred for that little girl. How I hate her."

"Why do you hate her?"

"After what I just told you about her, you can't honestly say that you think she's amazing."

"I know she's amazing, or you wouldn't be sitting here now."

"Yeah, right. I hate this therapeutic crap."

"Michelle, can you pause for a moment and help me understand what's behind your anger? What's driving the anger you feel?"

Michelle knew what the anger was hiding, but there was no way she wanted Dr. Natalie to know. Dr. Natalie already knew enough to no longer respect Michelle as a person and as a colleague. If Michelle told her any more, then their relationship would be over.

"It's okay, Michelle. You can tell me. You're safe here. There's no judgment here." Michelle knew that Dr. Natalie wasn't judging her. She was the judge, prosecutor, and jury. She was the one condemning little Michelle.

Dr. Natalie and Michelle sat in silence for a long time, as Michelle's anger mixed with intensifying tears. As the flood slowed, Michelle softly spoke. "Why do I feel anger now when back then I did not feel such, Dr. Natalie? I hate the fact that, at times, I wanted her and them to do what they did. Instead of being beat, I was . . ."

"You were what, Michelle?"

"Nothing. Never mind."

"Michelle, I need you to say it. You need to say it."

"I was touched, and it didn't hurt."

Amid the silence, truth and then calm entered the room. Michelle had said out loud what needed to be said. Both Dr. Natalie and Michelle sat silent with their personal tears reverencing the moment. Then in a soft voice to offer love, respect, and understanding, Dr. Natalie noted, "Michelle, I can't imagine how hard it was for you to share that. I know you blame little Michelle, but let me ask you this: what would you tell a client if they shared with you what you've just shared?"

"It doesn't matter what I'd tell clients. I'm not like other clients. I knew that what I felt was wrong."

"Wrong? No, all you wanted was to be loved and touched. Any child who was treated the way you were treated would have responded to such touching. You wanted to and needed to be loved. You did nothing wrong. I know that you would never tell a client they were ugly, bad, or wrong."

Michelle lowered her head to her hands and sobbed. Through love and understanding, Dr. Natalie had opened a very difficult lock. Now, instead of stuffing memories back into the box, Michelle allowed the healing power of tears to begin guiding sorrow toward truth. Michelle cried for a long time. It felt both comforting and safe for Michelle to cry in Dr. Natalie's office.

As their session closed that night, Dr. Natalie noted, "I hope there are many more tears to come over the next few days. There is so much you need to cry for."

"I know. All my life, I've cried alone. If more tears are to come, I'd prefer they come here in your office."

"I can understand that. How about we set another appointment for this week? Is that okay with you?"

At this point, Michelle wanted to say both yes and no. She knew her heart was changing and that for progress to continue, more boxes needed to open. Michelle also knew that the contents of the box they had just opened would take a while for her to completely process. Perhaps one more session would allow additional healing time before the next box came into view. It was also possible that one more session would help them both know what box Michelle needed to open next.

That night as Michelle drove home, she paid little attention to the world around her. Her heart was still bleeding from shame and guilt as she continued to process what she had shared in Dr. Natalie's office and what Dr. Natalie had said to her.

Maybe, just maybe, she was not such a horrible person, and maybe, just maybe, she could start to see little Michelle in a different light. Darkness was shifting, and Michelle had felt Dr. Natalie's love penetrate through in such a way that both little Michelle and the adult Michelle had felt it. "Thank you, God. Thank you," were the thoughts rolling over and over in Michelle's mind. She was healing. This night there was no call to Ivan. This night Michelle wanted just between her, Dr. Natalie, and God. This night little Michelle was in full view, and she wanted more truth told, more boxes opened, more understanding, and more love.

CHAPTER 10

The Last Content in the Third Box

A healing quest is best taken with a friend. A friend can offer love and hope while holding up a mirror to see truth. When you decide to embark on the healing quest, reach out and invite someone to talk to you after each session and remind you that you can make it through at least one more session of therapy.

WORK THIS MORNING WAS UNPRODUCTIVE, SO MICHELLE GAVE UP. SHE decided that a good cup of tea was just what she needed. As Michelle entered the Tea House and ordered a peach herbal tea, multiple thoughts raged—thoughts about what she had shared in her last session and about what box to unlock next.

Michelle desperately wanted deeper understanding and closure regarding what she had shared in her previous session. Michelle longed to be okay with Dr. Natalie knowing her dark secrets. The little Michelle wanted to explore deeper into the darkness. The adult Michelle desired no further exploration. The adult Michelle still strongly held to the belief that little Michelle was damaged and guilty. Michelle needed little Michelle to step back and get out of the way so that she and Dr. Natalie could get this journey over with, so that she could get back to peaceful nights, so that she didn't have to keep playing tug-of-war. Little Michelle needed the adult Michelle to get out of the way. She wanted to feel more love, and she had more stories to tell Dr. Natalie. Michelle looked at the clock. She had three hours to kill before her next appointment. Michelle had three hours to sit with her own introspections.

By what Michelle is sure was divine intervention, her phone rang. Dr. Natalie was calling to let Michelle know that her corporate review had been canceled and that she could see her now if Michelle was open to moving their appointment. "Yes, now would be great. I'm about twenty minutes away. Will that work?"

"Yes. I'll be in my office doing paperwork. Come on up when you arrive."

The concept of time is an interesting puzzle. When you want something, time seems to freeze, and when you'd prefer to avoid an event, time accelerates. In what seemed like only a few minutes, Michelle was climbing the stairs to Dr. Natalie's office. "One more time," she thought. "One more time." Michelle selected the seat closest to Dr. Natalie. Michelle needed to feel her presence. She needed to make sure there was no awkwardness between them after their last session. It was important to discern that Dr. Natalie genuinely believed what she had said, that she wasn't merely providing lip service. After all, Michelle was still blaming little Michelle. Did Dr. Natalie also blame little Michelle?

"How are you, Michelle?"

"In truth, I've been better. I'm having a hard time reining in thoughts. Because I have been unable to focus, I left work and went to a tea shop. I was dreading waiting three hours before our session. So, I'm glad we could meet sooner."

"I'm glad that meeting now works for both of us. Our last session was painful yet healing, and I want to know if you're okay."

"I think I am. I'm still struggling with the reality that you now know my dark deeds, but it is what it is."

"Michelle, there's no judgment here. I don't see anything dark. I see one of the most incredible people I have ever met. I see courage, not weakness, in you. You are the one who thinks you're to blame for what happened, and holding that view is so unfair to little Michelle."

"Okay, Dr. Natalie, I believe you hold no condemnation. So, where do we start today?"

"During our last session, you suggested that the reason you hate her so much is because she responded when her abusers sexually touched her. You also indicated that you hated little Michelle because sometimes she needed and wanted those sexual touches. I was thinking we should explore those thoughts further."

Dr. Natalie's words ripped open the final contents of the box they had been going through during their previous session. Michelle was speechless. All she wanted to do was to run—fast. Michelle jumped to her feet and walked to the far corner of Dr. Natalie's office. She kept her back to Dr. Natalie. Michelle needed space. She needed to escape. She needed to . . . She had no idea what she needed at the moment, but it was not talking about what Dr. Natalie had just brought up.

"Michelle, it's normal for a child to respond when touched sexually. We are biologically wired to respond, which is why sexual relations between two people who love each other are so powerful. You know this." Michelle heard Dr. Natalie but wasn't interested. Michelle felt like she couldn't breathe. The office was too small. Michelle couldn't get far enough away.

Dr. Natalie had just replaced the box with little Michelle, and at that moment, Michelle much more preferred boxes. Dr. Natalie wanted her to see little Michelle, feel her, and accept that Michelle's actions were normal considering the environment she was raised in. Little Michelle was asking for kindness and, if possible, love.

Michelle had no desire to comprehend what Dr. Natalie was saying. Michelle wanted to hold on to her interpretation. Michelle was ugly, and because of that deformity, the next box they needed to open containing twisted content could make sense. If Michelle wasn't hideous, then the deformities in the next box Dr. Natalie and Michelle needed to examine would not find resolution but only condemnation.

In anger and in hopes of escape, Michelle turned toward Dr. Natalie. "Michelle is broken. What she did . . . what she wanted . . . isn't right. It isn't normal. You have no idea!"

"Please enlighten me."

"No, you don't need enlightenment!"

Michelle returned to the couch and sat down, defeated. Tears and anger spilled forward. "Do you have any idea what I did? No, you don't."

"So, tell me, Michelle. What am I not seeing?" Again, Dr. Natalie and Michelle sat in silence. Dr. Natalie knew that Michelle needed to completely empty the box from their last session and to bring into the room a new box that was somehow tied to the other one.

"Dr. Natalie, when I was little, the abuse happened not just between males and females and between grown-ups and kids but also between females and females and between kids and kids. What happened between the males and females, whether they were adults or kids, always involved force. Perpetrators compelled their victims to do things they didn't want to do." With tears streaming down Michelle's face, she continued. "Dr. Natalie, the abuse between females and kids and between kids and other kids were the most confusing and hardest for me to understand both then and now. It was not forced. It was . . ." Michelle went silent.

"It was what, Michelle?" Michelle remained silent. "It's okay to say. I'm right here, and I'm not leaving."

"It felt okay and yet confusing."

"I bet it did. You were a little kid. You were trying to survive a horrific environment. An environment that ninety percent of the time was cruel. So, when there were touches that were not vicious, I'm sure that they felt different and that the little you might have wanted those moments. That's okay. There were no correct boundaries in your childhood."

"If I wanted to have any privileges as a child, I had to be the one who initiated sexual acts. I had to be the one who said I wanted it. That's why the little Michelle is so horrible. She felt something when she was touched by specific individuals, and she also willingly did what her guards wanted. So, when you ask me to see her as the victim, how can I, knowing what I know? There's no victim here."

Michelle's gaze moved to the floor. She couldn't look at Dr. Natalie. Dr. Natalie knew too much. Yet, somehow, Michelle knew that she'd still care about and respect her.

"Michelle, thank you for taking that risk and sharing with me. I know that doing so was painful, and I want you to recognize that I hold no judgment. What you've shared makes sense considering all that I know about your childhood. It's disheartening that you blame yourself. You were trying to survive. I also know that if our roles were reversed, with you as the doctor and me as the client, you'd convey a message similar to mine. You aren't bad. Bad things happened to you, and acting out and feeling sexual desires was your way to survive."

Part of Michelle wanted to disagree with Dr. Natalie, yet Michelle knew she was right. Through tears, Michelle said, "There's another box connected to this one that we need to talk about."

"Yes, we'll get to that box tomorrow." Michelle looked up, somewhat puzzled that today's session was apparently over. "Yes, tomorrow," Dr. Natalie said. "I know you're a sprinting client, but right now we need to slow the process to give you time to feel and to heal." There were tears in both of their eyes.

Michelle knew that Dr. Natalie's concern and caring were real. "Michelle, this is hard work, and you are so strong. Thank you for trusting me to take this journey with you. It's actually giving me time to consider a few things in my own life. I'm amazed at your strength. I promise you that we'll arrive at the finish line, but you need to remember that we're running a marathon, not an eight-hundred-meter sprint. The process will take time—more time than you want. But we're further along than I imagined possible, considering the abuse you experienced."

Both the adult and little Michelle shed tears. As the tears flowed, years of self-blame and acceptance were washing away, allowing both adult Michelle and little Michelle to accept love and understanding.

"Michelle, I'd like to give you an assignment now that we've emptied a few difficult boxes. I'd like you to write a letter, this time from little Michelle's perspective. I'd like little Michelle to write to you. I know that you're familiar with this therapy technique. Can you write this letter?"

"Sure. I'll give it a try."

"Great. I think we can end the session tonight and, Michelle, please remember to trust the process."

As Michelle entered her car, tears were flowing again. Michelle didn't feel like herself. Nevertheless, she cried tears of sorrow for all that was lost. Michelle also cried tears of forgiveness for both her young self and adult self. Intermingled with these tears were tears of self-doubt and fear, resulting from the assignment Dr. Natalie had given her.

There was too much to contemplate. Michelle needed a break. She called Ivan, and this time instead of reviewing what she had talked to Dr. Natalie about, she and Ivan decided to go to dinner and talk. How blessed Michelle was to have Ivan in her life. She needed him in this journey as much as she needed Dr. Natalie.

After dinner Michelle found herself once again in the safety of her car crossing miles as she considered the next letter Dr. Natalie had asked her to write. "I have given my own clients such an assignment but never myself. I am not even sure how to start," Michelle said out loud to her empty car space. "This is so different. Being the client really makes one think about what clients are asked to do. I guess I just need to visualize a little girl about the age I was and start writing. Hopefully in the process of writing the story will unfold and little Michelle will be able to tell me what she needs me to hear. If not, then I know I'll get stuck with the assignment of rewriting, and I would rather not have to do this twice. Man, this is taking so much longer than I wanted, but I guess that is okay. I can tell I am healing, and I know Dr. Natalie is a competent psychologist. We will get there and I will stay to the end."

Just then Michelle's phone rang, and she welcomed Ivan's call as a disruption to the weighty thoughts in her mind. "Hey, stranger, didn't I just see you?"

"Yes, but you didn't tell me how your session went. So how did it go?"

"Hard. Always hard."

"That is exactly what I wanted to hear."

"You know, Ivan, I think you and Dr. Natalie are working together against me."

"No, not at all. We are working for you."

"Funny, my friend, that is funny."

"Yes, I know you are and I love you too. So what did Dr. Natalie ask you to do this time?"

"I have to let little Michelle write a letter to me."

"Oh, that sounds interesting. How are you going to do that?"

"I have no idea. Somehow I have to become a child again."

"Cool, that's not hard at all. Just come hang out with me. I love being a child. I know you don't but I do. This is going to be hard for you."

"Yes, Ivan, it will be just like it always is. You would think I could have just one session that was easy, but no."

"Oh, my friend, if it was easy it would not be you. Ever since I have known you, you have never done anything the easy way. If it was easy you would not do it."

"And you call me your friend. Maybe I need to get a new best friend."

"Oh, you love me and you know it. You worship the quicksand I walk on."

"Thanks, Ivan, have a good night."

"I would tell you to do the same, but then a letter would not be written."

"Night, Ivan!"

"Night, Michelle, talk to you tomorrow."

"And as always, call me if the letter writing gets to be too heavy."

"Deal."

As Michelle hung up the phone, the tasks before her weighed in and she knew it would be a long night. She also knew there would be no call to Ivan. This she had to do alone, no matter how dark or how long it took. She knew little Michelle had a message for her.

CHAPTER 11

The Fourth Box:
Tears Released

True therapy offers healing to the whole person. Tender, mending mercies are applied to the past, the present, and the future. This process of wholeness reaches the deepest depths and the highest heights, bringing tears of sorrow but also tears of joy.

THAT NIGHT, INSTEAD OF SLEEPING MICHELLE COMPOSED TWO LETTERS AS SHE shed healing tears through the words and thoughts of little Michelle. As she entered Dr. Natalie's office the next morning, Michelle felt lighter, as though thousands of pounds had been lifted from her heart. Locks were opening, and Michelle felt more prepared to review the letters she had drafted during the night.

"Good morning, Michelle. I'm glad we could make this morning work. I think it's important that you're back in my office today. We need to continue moving forward in these complex areas. I worried that if we let the weekend arrive before completing this chapter, that lid might slam shut, never to be opened again."

Michelle nodded in agreement.

"So, tell me about your night."

"I spent the night in tears. Similar to another night I experienced not so long ago, but this time the tears I cried were directed by the composition of letters." Michelle knew that as a child, she had cried herself to sleep multiple times. The tears she had cried last night, although based in sorrow, allowed her to feel and mourn the abused little Michelle. The tears helped replace loss with hope. This growing hope was allowing Michelle's perceptions of her younger self to shift from hatred to neutrality. Michelle's disapproval and shame were surrendering to acceptance and understanding. Michelle was not all the way there yet, but she was moving in the right direction.

"This might seem strange, but last night's tears felt like a warm blanket of comfort. As a young child, when I was at Auntie Vi's house and needed to take a nap, she'd place me on her bed and cover me with a soft, wonderful quilt. I considered it a magic quilt because it was warm on cool days and cool on warm days. I loved feeling that quilt wrapped around me, and last night some of my tears wrapped a little girl in understanding and love."

"That's powerful. Thank you for sharing. Maybe you need to find a similar quilt for yourself now."

"I think that's a great idea." (A few weeks later Michelle purchased her quilt.)

"Michelle, your journey has been very powerful so far. I know I won't be the same because of it, and I think you're beginning to see that you've changed as well. Healing is hard work and a spiritual process. I gave you the assignment last night to let little Michelle write a letter to adult Michelle. Before we review that letter, I'd like to share a few thoughts, if that's okay with you. I know that you're a very competent, determined, and faith-filled individual. I also know that each of these qualities can sometimes become a barrier in the healing process. I'm impressed with your willingness to embrace these more intense aspects of therapy like writing letters, painting pictures, and talking about painful events even when at first you're resistant. Today, I'm hoping that we can let grown-up Michelle take a step back and just let the little Michelle talk. I think that allowing her to share will help guide you. She's not broken; she's not ugly; she's not at fault. She's a survivor, and today I need you to let her share."

Michelle hoped that her letters accomplished what Dr. Natalie was looking for. Michelle was learning that it was easier to talk about the events of her childhood than to picture herself as a child. Michelle also understood, as a mental health practitioner, how important inner childhood work is in the healing process. Michelle never in her wildest dreams imagined she would be the one asked, as a client, to participate in this empty-chair process.

"Are you ready to read the letter?"

"Yes. I actually wrote two letters. If it's okay with you, I'd like to read each of them."

"I'm good with that."

"The first letter may seem odd, but it contains the verbal exchange I had with little Michelle as I shed tears last night."

ADULT MICHELLE

Michelle, why is it through uncontrollable tears of sorrow and grief that I finally see you? I see you not as I chose to define you but as you truly are. Why is it that within these tears I engage in the final step of accepting you? Why is it your pain that breaks my facade and sets you free? Why, when all your life you cried alone, do I find myself once again in that all-too-familiar place, curled up, alone, and sobbing? This is so not what I wanted. Why now? Yes, I know. It is now, for in truth this healing process is between me and you guided by God and Dr. Natalie. It is our tears that must mix so together we can let go and find peace. It is I who must now mourn for you when no one else did.

Oh, Michelle, I don't know how to stop these tears. I don't know how to comfort you. I don't know how to keep you safe. I don't know how to love you. I don't know what to do. It hurts. It hurts so deep. Please make it stop. Please make it go away. I don't think I'm strong enough to face what you faced and to feel what you felt. Michelle, I'm so sorry for how deeply your family hurt you and that they never loved you. Please, Michelle, please make this sadness go away. Please just hold me. I feel so alone. I feel so lost. I am so scared. I don't think I'm strong enough, but I know you are.

LITTLE MICHELLE

It's okay. You don't have to be strong. You just have to be real. It's okay to cry. Yes, it hurts, but the tears will stop, and you'll make it one more day. You're strong. You're a survivor. You're brave, and you do love me. You need me. You just don't know it all the way yet. There are people who love you and care about you. You just need to be a little better at letting them in and letting them know you need them and that you might hurt once in a while.

ADULT MICHELLE

Please make the tears stop. I can't take this type of pain. Dr. Natalie told me many times that the tears would come but that they would also stop and not last forever.

LITTLE MICHELLE

Michelle, I've needed you to cry like this for so long. I've needed you to heal. This is so right, and this is so good. I love you, and this is what you need. Yes, it hurts, but tears heal. I promise they heal.

ADULT MICHELLE

Heal what?

LITTLE MICHELLE

They heal us. You can see that we aren't broken. We were never broken. We were abused, and we survived. We're strong, we're safe, and we can do anything. It's okay to be authentic. You need and deserve to be loved. Please stop seeing us as broken. Please see us as whole. I survived. You survived. We survived. And now you are truly ready to be loved in ways you've never been loved before. It's time to stop running. Open your heart; it's okay to do so. As you accept what you feel and want, you'll find wholeness. I'm whole and can help you be whole too.

"Michelle, thank you for that," Dr. Natalie said. "It's powerful to hear what little Michelle had to say. I especially liked the fact that you allowed little Michelle to respond and try to comfort you. She is wise and I can tell that she has a bit to teach you. I'm sure you know this type of inner child work can be a helpful part of therapy, and I'm excited that you allowed yourself to go there. How do you feel after writing this letter?"

"This letter allowed tears to flow more freely, and I think it prepared me to write the second letter. I also recognize that this letter exposed the vulnerability of the adult Michelle."

"I agree, and it's nice to see such depth and honesty. Well done. You are indeed doing hard work. I am both impressed and deeply moved. It has been a long time since a client of mine has been willing to do such deep emotional healing."

Michelle knew it was now time to read the second letter.

TO THE ADULT MICHELLE

Michelle, thank you, thank you for yesterday. Thank you for finally— oh my gosh—telling Dr. Natalie. I'm so proud of you; you aren't a chicken anymore. Wow, guess what? When you told Dr. Natalie, she didn't leave. She still loves you! She didn't think you were terrible.

I knew it was going to be okay. For far too long, you hated yourself. You thought you hated me, but guess what? It's not me you hated. I'm okay with all that I did. I'm not the bad kid. I'm the good kid. I made it so that you could be here, and I like you. Maybe now you can start to love me and you.

It's okay to feel, to want, to need, and to be close to people—good people, I mean. I have known way too many bad ones, but they're gone now. Well, almost gone. Michelle, you can let people in. You can let me in. I'm singing. Can you hear me? I'm no longer alone. Yes, yes, yes! I'm so happy! Woo-hoo! You did it. Yes, yes, yes.

Michelle, weep. But not for me. You need to cry for you. I know that if you can just let the tears go, I can leave that trailer and you'll see me right next to you and a part of all that's good.

Hey, older me. What you need to understand is that I was and am amazing. Trust me—I can do stuff other little girls can't do. Because of me, you like to fish, hike, and do other things outdoors. Outdoor activities were both my escape and where I built and increased my strength to deal with the bad stuff. Outside hidden in the trees I was safe. It's so cool that with just a stick and some line you can have your own personal fishing pole. Not fancy but it worked. Auntie Vi taught me that. Mom couldn't take away sticks. Because of me, you love people as profoundly as you do. You're the one who needed to cry, and guess what? You did for a while. Crying is a good, but trust me that it's nothing compared to what still needs to come.

Stop turning off the tears. I want to yell at you and stomp my feet when you do that. Just cry, please. Or are you still too chicken? It'll be so great when you do let yourself cry for as long as is needed. I know, I know you think you have cried, but you and I both know you shut them down way to soon. If you let me, I can help you grieve. Okay, what else do you need me to tell you? I think you're a superstar, but don't let that go to your head.

Did you know that Dr. Natalie has a really hard name to say? What kind of name is Stachowski? Oh, and by the way, will you tell Dr. Natalie how amazing I think she is? Tell her how much I love her. When you open up, I see the tears in her eyes, and I like that; it makes me feel safe and loved. No one has ever cried for me. Michelle, we are going to be okay, and I think you're starting to know that. Now promise me that you'll finish. You are so close, and I want out of the trailer.
—Little Michelle

"Michelle, what a great letter. Thank you for sharing. Little Michelle really understands the journey we are on. I like the little you. I know you do not, but I sure do. She is one of the reasons you are so strong. How do you feel after writing this letter?"

"I can say that I am starting to see little Michelle differently. I'm not as far as I need to be, but I know I'll get there. I also know the value of the written assignments I've completed. Thank you. These letters are not so easy to write, but clearly, they created a path for unlocking bolts. I'm gaining respect for little Michelle. I still have many questions for her, or I guess I should say 'us,' in this therapy process."

"Yes, I'm sure you do. I want to give myself an assignment. I'm going to write a letter to little Michelle. Is that okay with you? And then may I share it with you? I'd also like you to continue writing. I think it's very therapeutic for you. As you write, focus on the words you haven't spoken yet during our sessions but want to. I'm not sure what those words are, but I think you do. Also, if you find it hard to write you can try using art. Many times clients find self-expression and emotional release through art. This week has been full of growth and healing. You faced some pretty big mountains and, from my perspective, made it to the top. Reaching the top doesn't mean these mountains are conquered, but it does mean they are starting to give. I agree with little Michelle. I think many more tears will come. I think we should set three appointments for next week, and if we don't need all of them, we can just cancel them. I'd rather have them set than try to fit them into our challenging schedules."

Michelle nodded in agreement, though not sure she wanted three more heavy sessions. At the same time, Michelle wanted to reach the end of this journey. As Michelle prepared to leave Dr. Natalie's office, their typical handshake was replaced with a momentary embrace. As they released, Michelle offered a humble thank-you.

Dr. Natalie replied, "You're welcome, Michelle."

As Michelle drove home, a few tears fell—not out of pain but out of love. Michelle loved Dr. Natalie, and she knew Dr. Natalie loved her. They were sharing a sacred bond. Michelle let several miles pass before calling Ivan, not wanting to disrupt the sacredness of her embrace with Dr. Natalie.

"So how did it go?"

"It was good. I can tell that there is progress, and it is such a sacred privilege to take this journey with Dr. Natalie. I know she truly cares, and what is really wonderful, Ivan, is that I can feel her love. I know although this is her job that Dr. Natalie loves me as a person and has great empathy for my life experiences."

"I am sure she does, and I think it is so cool you can feel her love. I love the softer side you are now allowing me and Dr. Natalie to see. It's nice that Dr. Chambers takes a break once in a while."

"You know, Ivan, you have told me that before, that I am Dr. Chambers with you. I really do not try to be, and don't want to be with you."

"I know that, and it is okay because I am Ivan and I have known you forever, so you trust me. But with most people you are Dr. Chambers, and you don't need to be. You are so amazing, and you have such a good heart. You just need to let more people see that. Just like you have let me, and you are letting Dr. Natalie. I am so proud of you. I know this is not easy work, but I can see a difference in you. Your walls are not as thick, and you are starting to relax just a little. Of course we wouldn't want you to go too far. You know we wouldn't want to you have to go talk to your religious leader, but then maybe . . ."

"Funny, Ivan, you are too funny. I love you too. Thank you for being my sounding board during this process."

Michelle's conversation with Ivan that night wasn't filled with frustration or sorrow but with admiration and respect for Dr. Natalie, a gracious individual who was willing to travel a treacherous road so that a childhood filled with sexual, physical, and emotional abuse could be uncovered by healing.

CHAPTER 12

Letters Shared

Even in the darkest hell, light finds a way in if the wounded soul is willing to light a wick with someone else's candle. The resulting illumination can be shared with others.

To help you as the reader navigate this chapter, I have taken the liberty to offer a few explanations. In therapy it can be a common practice to participate in letter writing as a means to processing traumatic events. Letter writing is a way in which the adult client can connect with their child self. It is also a medium for both client and psychologist to express thoughts and feelings, and to identify progress.

In this chapter Dr. Natalie shared her letter with the client Michelle. After hearing Dr. Natalie's letter, Michelle writes a first response to Dr. Natalie's letter from the perspective of adult Michelle and is then invited to write a second response from the perspective of little Michelle. In this chapter you will first read Dr. Natalie's letter followed by Michelle's first and second responses to each of the main thoughts of Dr. Natalie's letter.

DR. NATALIE AND MICHELLE OPENED THEIR NEXT SESSION BY RECOUNTING what they did over the weekend. Michelle's weekend had been relaxing. She hadn't even thought about what boxes she would open next. Michelle let Dr. Natalie's office float to the back of her mind as she enjoyed time with her four children. Dr. Natalie spent her weekend moving, which was not so fun.

"Where shall we start today, Michelle?"

"I think you had an assignment that you need to report back on. It was nice to be out of the hot seat."

"Yes, I wrote a letter to little Michelle. May I share it with you?"

"That would be great." Michelle was very interested to hear what Dr. Natalie had written to little Michelle.

Dear Michelle,

First of all, thank you for sharing with me what you wrote. I know that writing such things is very scary, and I'm honored that you felt safe enough to share them with me.

You need to know that you're a very brave girl. Being brave doesn't mean you don't cry or you don't feel afraid. It means you keep trying and keep facing each day no matter how many tears have fallen and no matter how scary life becomes.

I wish that an angel could show you a vision of what your life will someday look like. I know that you often wonder if you'll even survive. Well, I know that you'll survive—and not only survive but become a strong, beautiful person who builds an amazing life. Your life will be filled with accomplishments, but even more important, you'll create peace and safety for your children. In part because of the sad and scary things you've gone through, you'll make sure that your children never go through anything like that. You'll be a wonderful, loving mother and not anything like Julie, the woman who raised you. You'll also show kindness to everyone around you. Others will turn to you for advice as well as support because of the way you respect their feelings and show love and care.

You need to know that the way Julie treated you is not the behavior of a mother or someone who deserves to be called a mother. There are rules and even laws for grown-ups about how they can treat their children. It's true! Grown-ups aren't supposed to hurt their children, neither their physical bodies nor their souls. Grown-ups are supposed to respect children's privacy and not touch them in ways that make them feel scared or confused. Grown-ups shouldn't even let children see things that make them feel this way.

Most mothers and fathers know these rules by nature, but there are laws to try to protect kids whose parents don't know or don't care about these rules.

There are also laws that say parents are supposed to take care of their kids, such as by making sure they always have enough food, a safe place to live, clothes, and other necessities. Children are supposed to go to school—that's even a law! There are many other things kids need that aren't specified in laws but that good parents try to make sure their children have, such as friends, things to play with, and chances to learn about the world in a safe way.

Sometimes people aren't able or willing to take care of a child the way they're supposed to. Maybe they're too sick and have to stay in bed all day, or maybe they're sad or angry all the time and don't know how to take care of a child. Nevertheless, they're supposed to make sure that their child is taken care of by someone who can do all the things that a good parent does. Sometimes grown-ups have a child they don't want or can't care for, and they give the child to someone who wants to be a mom or a dad.

If a child is being hurt, grown-ups who know about it are responsible for making sure that the child gets help so he or she can be safe and healthy. Even though grown-ups knew about what was happening to you, it doesn't mean that what was happening was okay. They were wrong in not keeping you safe.

The most important thing is what you already know: We are all God's children. Good moms and dads know that they don't own a child; a child isn't his or her parents' property, and they can't do whatever they want with the child. Parents are only stewards, entrusted with a little person put on earth. Parents' job is to help their child grow and learn until the child can take care of himself or herself. If parents don't keep their child safe or if they do things that hurt the child's body or soul, they are mistreating one of God's children. If parents fail to fulfill their responsibility to care for their child— for any reason at all—the child has the right to choose a different family.

In your lifetime, you'll meet special people who see who you really are, and they'll love you without expecting anything in return. They'll be part of your "heart family" and will help you heal from the hurt and confusion that was created during your years with the family you were born into. I'm so lucky that I met you and that I'm able to help you on this difficult journey of healing. I care about you and want you to be able to experience and enjoy the wonderful things that life can offer. At the same time that I'm helping you, you're helping me on my journey.

It's hard to verbalize such confusing things, but I hope this letter is of some help in explaining how you deserve to be treated. Of course, you can ask me about anything you have questions about!

With love,
Dr. Natalie

Tears flowed down Michelle's face. No one else had ever written such a letter to her. Michelle felt loved. She felt understood. She felt heard. She felt guided. Dr. Natalie knew most of Michelle's deep dark secrets and didn't run away; she didn't shut her out, or ignore her, or tell her she was bad, or make fun of her. Instead Dr. Natalie allowed all the ugliness of Michelle's childhood into the office to be examined, explained, and then released while offering professional guidance, love, understanding, and support. Dr. Natalie made it safe for Michelle to heal through the expression of emotions. She allowed Michelle to be the lost little girl pleading for love and understanding and responded to that pleading so that the silence of an abusive childhood was finally broken, thus giving to Michelle the gift of complete trust. Dr. Natalie's letter was addressed to the little Michelle in the room, but it was the adult Michelle who was feeling these emotions. Dr. Natalie handed Michelle the letter, and she cradled it in her hands. It was a precious gift to be kept and reread in the weeks and years to come.

"Thank you, Dr. Natalie. I don't know what else to say." In truth, Michelle wanted to say more, but as a therapist herself she recognized the importance of keeping boundaries between client and counselor. Michelle wanted to thank Dr. Natalie not only for being her guide but also for loving her during the process. Michelle wanted to say that she loved her too, but now was not the time. Perhaps one day the time would come for such a sincere disclosure.

"Dr. Natalie, I'd like to end our session here today to allow me a few days to write a response to your letter if that's okay with you."

"Yes, that would be great. I look forward to reading little Michelle's response."

Michelle left Dr. Natalie's office that day with her letter in hand, feeling loved and cared for in ways that words fail to explain. There was no longer a thin wall between Dr. Natalie and Michelle but instead a very deep and personal level of acceptance. Dr. Natalie's letter was given freely with no strings attached. Dr. Natalie's letter allowed Michelle to know Dr. Natalie's heart and mind and to see that she really did not judge her nor consider her damaged but instead desired for her to know love. Dr. Natalie encouraged Michelle to allow others in as part of her heart family. This letter removed any emotional distance between Michelle and Dr. Natalie. The expression of Dr. Natalie's thoughts in the form of a letter assisted Michelle in feeling truly loved by another person. Michelle was excited to write her response and to return and share it in their next session.

As Michelle entered Dr. Natalie's office for their next appointment, she handed Dr. Natalie her letter of response.

MICHELLE'S FIRST RESPONSE

Dr. Natalie,

I know I won't be able to adequately express how sensitively and powerfully your letter penetrated my thoughts and feelings. I also know that a thank-you will never adequately acknowledge the respect and gratitude I hold for you. How insightful that Heavenly Father placed you in my life many years ago. He's again brought you into my life, knowing I needed the changes you've helped me make. There are many great women I've had the privilege of calling friends. Know that I count you as one of the greatest among these women. I also will consider it a sacred privilege to refer to you as a good friend when the time is appropriate to do so.

You helped create that safety. I've known for quite some time that I was safe to share with you my deepest thoughts and emotions, as well as my darkest experiences. I knew you'd never judge me but would comfort, encourage, and love. You've offered me a sacred gift.

The other day, Joy, a dear friend of mine, said the following: "I've known very few individuals who've been committed to taking the journey you and Dr. Natalie have taken. Many start, but most quit. You've healed in so many ways and are so far ahead emotionally of so many of us. That's because of who you are, who Dr. Natalie is, and who she is to you. Have you ever thought about the name you hold? There's a reason you hold it. God has been there in your life, and you trust Him just as Michelle of old did. Thus, you trust Dr. Natalie."

Ivan asked the other day as we talked about the journey you and I have taken, "How are you ever going to date? You're successful, and now you're so emotionally whole that every guy you meet is going to be even more intimidated. I love the new and softer side of Michelle. You've always been amazing, but now I can't even tell you how much more amazing you are. I wish I could meet this Dr. Natalie. She's been such a gift and godsend in your life."

With tears in my eyes, I responded, "She sure has!"

I'm trying to see this truth more each day. I know there's a voice that still haunts at moments. The voice has driven me to do more to prove I'm good enough. That voice has quieted, and now I hear it only when I feel lost and alone or when some of my past comes rushing forward. Thank you.

Thank you for using the name Julie instead of the word "mother." Julie was never a mother but more like a stranger. As a mother, I've made a lot of mistakes. It's hard learning to be a mom when your only example was what a mother shouldn't be, but I've been blessed by my children. They're forgiving, and I love them deeply. I know that they know I love them.

Dr. Natalie, there's a box that's still closed. I've danced around it many times. I can't keep dancing. I need help in opening this box, and I think I'm ready—at least, I hope I am. This box is tied to my past and my present. This Christmas season has been rather rough, and I've longed for the safety of your office. I'd say I'm going backward, but I know that's not true. My feelings are more poignant, more real. There are no more surface emotions.

It's difficult to admit that a lot was missing in my childhood. There were times when I wished my parents would've given me away. I don't think I've ever told you this, but often I wanted my parents to just let me die. It's clear that my parents didn't want me. I'm not sure if they even want me now. That doesn't matter. I no longer need them in the role of parents. There are others in my life I now consider to be mothers to me.

Auntie Vi tried to do that for a few days out of the year. How blessed I was to be her little Shelly. Side note: I would never let anyone else call me that—just her.

It's just so hard for a little girl to accept that everyone who was supposed to keep her safe and to love her chose not to. At moments, I just want to scream. What was wrong with all of you? Why didn't you love me? I was just a little kid. All I wanted was for you to love me. All I needed was love. I didn't need packages or birthday parties (neither of which I got). I just wanted you to love me.

In regard to a heart family, I think I'm starting to choose mine. Barbara, a longtime friend, loves me the way a mother should. We talked on Christmas Day, and I can't tell you the joy I felt in my soul as I heard her voice and she reminded me of how much she loved me. I'm having lunch with her New Year's Day. I'd like you to meet her. Would you be open to doing that?

I hope this doesn't make you uncomfortable, but I think you are part of that heart family, as are Barbara and Joy.

When the time is right, I look forward to hearing far more about your life journey.

I want you to know how much I love and respect you.
—Michelle

"Michelle, I appreciate your response to this letter. There's great insight in your words, but they're the words of adult Michelle, not little Michelle. I was hoping you'd let little Michelle answer the letter since I addressed my letter to her." Dr. Natalie was right. The adult Michelle had responded on behalf of the little Michelle. Dr. Natalie continued, "I think little Michelle might have written a completely different response. Can you write another reply and this time let little Michelle respond?"

Michelle nodded. "I'd thought we were done with the inner child work. Apparently not. You know, Dr. Natalie, I get the purpose of this inner child work—I really do—but at times you are pushing the envelope a little bit in your requests. I am not sure if you know this or not, but there are moments when I leave your office and in the soundproof space of my car share a few verbal 'what the hell is she thinking' moments. In my head I see myself telling you I quit at least a thousand times, threatening never to return. Can't you just be okay with this letter and let it go? I am not sure I can dig any deeper. I just don't know how. I get that I am getting very close, but each time that closeness feels so emotionally overwhelming that I just shut down. Perhaps it is just too much, and maybe I am not as strong as you think I am. I just want to be done. Please, can we just be done?"

"Michelle, I am sure this is very hard, and I can understand why you want to be done. I wish we were done as well, but we agreed to the end. I don't think we are there yet, but I do think we are getting closer. You are stronger than you think, and from what I know of you I think strong enough to do what needs to be done. Let's finish this part, one more letter for now anyway. You got this," Dr. Natalie said as her eyes glimmered and she offered a compassionate smile.

Michelle endured a few more sleepless nights as she allowed herself to walk back through prior blocked off memories of her childhood. She recalled such events as empty seats at her state championship basketball game and a leftover corsage for the mothers of the graduating seniors on the high school baseball team. The sneaking of a screwdriver from her dad's construction truck to see if a broken heater might be fixed. Making excuses as to why she could never go to the movies, or hang out after school, or why no one could come to her home. Making sure she always took gym class or played sports so that no more creek bathing was required. She recalled her first job at twelve years old helping an egg farmer down the road, Mr. Jameson, and how amazing it felt when she had enough money to buy her very first pair of Levi blue jeans. The joy she experienced when she thought that finally she could be like the other kids, but not even with Levi jeans, that she washed out every other day, was she ever going to be like the other kids. "No child should ever have to know the life I knew," Michelle mumbled. "No child."

MICHELLE'S SECOND RESPONSE

It's scary to write—to tell another person what only I know, what I'm not supposed to tell people about. The older Michelle wouldn't like me

75

talking about it. She has tried so hard to keep me quiet, but I think she is starting to like me and is okay with what I felt, what I did, and what happened to me. At the least, she's talking about it and not pretending it didn't happen. You need to help her feel deeper than she wants to feel. There are so many hurts left, and she needs to cry more, Dr. Natalie. She needs to get angry. Don't tell her I told you this, but she has a few more things she needs to tell you.

Dr. Stachowski (man that is a hard name to say), I think you know I cry a lot, but my tears never seem to stop the hurt. When I cry, my mom just gets madder. I cry alone. It's nice that you think I'm brave. I just think I'm scared. No one seems to see me unless they want to hurt me. It's scary. I don't know what to do.

I am glad you get to meet me when I am an adult and that you wish I could see now who I would become. I've never seen an angel, but I do talk to God. I bet you do as well. He knows me. I never want to hurt anyone. How cool that I'll have kids. I'll make sure they're loved and safe. I'll never hurt them, and they'll have a great Christmas each year. Do you like Christmas? I'm glad to know that I'll get out of here.

So, based on your words in your letter, my parents are breaking the rules. My parents are bad instead of me? Wow, that's cool! Why do the rules not protect me? Why don't my parents follow the rules? How come no one saves me? I guess maybe it's because I never tell anyone, but my Auntie Vi and Grandma know. Why are they quiet?

So, you say there are laws to protect me? Can I see these laws? My parents ignore the laws. It's cold at night, and there's no heat. I do get food, but I have to eat alone. I don't have any friends. Kids just make fun of me. I want someone to protect me. Can you?

At times, I wish that my parents would give me away, but then I wouldn't have a family. I want a family. I don't want my family to leave me. I just want them to be nice. Maybe they could learn to be nice. They say I do things that make them mad. I try really hard not to be bad, but I guess I still am, so my family hurts me. But if there are rules like you say, then the abuse isn't my fault—it's their fault. They need to learn to keep the rules. Then I won't get hurt.

I guess my whole family is broken and they don't keep the rules. Maybe they don't know the rules, but I bet they do. Why are they so broken?

I talk to God, and I think He loves me. It's hard to think about choosing a heart family because I want this one to love me, even though they don't. How can they not love a child? I guess I can think about choosing a heart family. I think that doing so might hurt, but it also might be nice to feel loved. I'd choose a mom who loved me. Who talked to me. Who would hold me. I would select a mom who didn't hurt me. A mom who saw me and who let me live in the house.

Thank you for telling me that people will love me and think I'm good. That they'll be kind to me, and I won't have to do anything that makes me uncomfortable. My current family makes me do stuff that makes me feel funny. I want to be loved. Is what they did to me love? I don't think so.

I'm glad you met me as an adult. It would have been nice if you'd met me when I was a child.

I'm glad I can ask you anything, and I know you won't hurt me.
—*Little Michelle*

"That's a much more connected response. It's interesting to hear the different perspectives. The adult you trends toward intellectual scripting, whereas the little you speaks from the heart. Would you agree with that?"

"Yes, I prefer the mental dialogue during therapy. It's safer."

"I'm not so sure it's safer, but it does allow you to keep the little Michelle locked away."

"Well, we both know you have been quite successful in shifting me out of my brain and into my heart. Part of me wants to be mad at you, while another part of me is so grateful. I know your guidance to shift me out of my brain and to look at the raw truth is helping me to heal. The writing of the letters, the painting, and the conversations in your office have allowed me to feel. Hard. Oh my gosh yes, but healing in ways I am not sure words can explain. I know my heart and soul are changing, Dr. Natalie. I feel lighter, I feel safer, I feel—I feel love and it feels good."

Dr. Natalie just smiled.

"In the response letter, little Michelle implied there are a few more boxes to unpack and more tears to shed. Do you agree?"

"You know, Dr. Natalie, I think I'm going to stop letting little Michelle talk to you. Perhaps she trusts you too much. Yes, there are a few more locked boxes—boxes that include not only my past but also my present. These boxes place condemnation at my feet, not at the feet of my abusers, and it's far harder for me to talk about what I did than what was done to me. These boxes are locked with shame, which developed because of my actions and some of my personal beliefs. I'm not sure I can explain some of the content."

"Michelle, you have a tendency to blame yourself, even when it's clear that the blame isn't justified. So, before we go too far down that road, how about we agree to look at the next box? Then we can decide together if you deserve to be convicted. I have no idea what experiences you're referring to, but based on what I do know of you, I have a hard time picturing you doing something so bad that you deserve such self-hatred."

Instead of replying out loud, Michelle only thought her response. "If I unlock the next box, you'll see that I'm right. You'll see."

"Well, Michelle, our time is up for the day, and I think this is a good place to stop. I'll see you Wednesday."

"Yes, you'll see me Wednesday," Michelle thought, "but not for box unlocking."

As Michelle drove home that night, her thoughts were engaged in a tug-of-war. She had started this journey for the purpose of complete healing. She had told herself that if Dr. Natalie agreed to the adventure, then she would see the quest to the end. She would not leave any item unexplored. But now, the last thing Michelle wanted to do was analyze the contents of the final boxes—boxes she had secured with locks of steel. How could she return to Dr. Natalie's office and finish their work together while leaving these last boxes sealed? Little Michelle was wrong. Michelle didn't need any more tears, and she didn't want to empty these boxes.

Michelle was scheduled to return to Dr. Natalie's office in two days. Michelle was positive that Dr. Natalie knew there were more boxes to open even before little Michelle had admitted it. Dr. Natalie had amazing spiritual insight. Michelle was also a person who had to tell the full truth. Michelle had tried revealing partial pieces in the past, and doing so left her with sleepless nights. What was she going to do now?

Michelle knew that if she called Ivan and told him her dilemma, he would be on Dr. Natalie's side. He would say that Michelle wouldn't be at peace until she had finished what she had started. He would remind her that Heavenly Father wanted her to finish this journey. Ivan would also tell Michelle that Dr. Natalie and he would love her no matter what was in the boxes.

No, Michelle definitely wasn't going to call Ivan. Instead, he called her. Michelle knew it wasn't a coincidence—God's hand had been involved. Sometimes, what you don't want is exactly what you need.

Reluctantly, Michelle answered the phone. "Hello."

"So, how did it go?"

"You know what, Ivan, I'm getting rather tired of this process, and I think Dr. Natalie and I have gone far enough. It's time to call it quits and for me to refocus on all the other items that are taking a back seat to this nightmare of a healing process."

"Nightmare, is it? I thought you and Dr. Natalie were making great progress, and now it is a nightmare. Why all the back sliding? I thought you were excited to share your letters with Dr. Natalie."

"Yes, I think part of me was ready to share the letters, but another part of me knew that when I read the letters such verbal offerings would pull a few more boxes into Dr. Natalie's view that I was working very hard to keep hidden."

"Oh, I see. Now you know there is still more work to do and you want to run away. Why, I can't imagine any boxes more arduous than the ones you have already opened."

"Well, trust me when I tell you that there are and that the boxes now on Dr. Natalie's radar are boxes I planned never to tell anyone, not even you. These are boxes of self-condemnation, and no one—and I mean, Ivan, *no one*—needs to know what is in them."

"Then why did you tell Dr. Natalie about them?"

"I didn't. Little Michelle did."

"Come again."

"In the letters I wrote as part of inner child work, little Michelle told Dr. Natalie that there were more boxes, but in truth I think she already knew."

"You know, Michelle, every box in your eyes is horrible, so why not just trust the process? You have so far. Trust and you may find out your next boxes are not any worse than the ones you have already opened."

"I wish you were right, Ivan. How I wish you were right, but I know what is in those boxes, not you and not Dr. Natalie."

"Well, my friend, I am sure you do, but I also know you—better than you know yourself at times. I know you will not quit. You will see this journey to the end because you love and respect Dr. Natalie and because you know it is time to heal from all of it. I also know you know God wants you to do this. There's so much He needs you to do, and your healing will open the doors to those opportunities. So, argue all you want. Quit all you want. Yell all you want. I know you will be back in Dr. Natalie's office whenever your next appointment is."

"You know, Ivan, sometimes I dislike you."

"Yes, but you love me always."

"Ivan, my next appointment isn't until Wednesday. It's not like I'll have only one difficult night before I talk to Dr. Natalie."

"Okay, then cry for two nights and one day. Get your pride out of the way. Do what you know, deep in your heart, you want to do."

"Yeah, right. You think you're funny. I'll talk to you tomorrow."

"You may not like me right now, but you love me. Good night."

As Michelle hung up the phone, the drama on the stage of her mind returned. How could anyone understand what was in the next box? Michelle was sure that Ivan's prediction about her crying throughout the night would be accurate. And this sleepless night would blend into difficult days of anger, tears, denial, and the desire to quit. On the one hand, Michelle's appointment with Dr. Natalie would not arrive fast enough; on the other hand, it would arrive too soon.

Michelle offered a silent prayer of gratitude to her Heavenly Father for consistently being a part of her life, even when she didn't listen to Him or want to do what He knew she needed to do. Given the terrible events of Michelle's childhood, people might ask why she believed that God had been with her during all her life. Michelle knew that God was loving, just, and merciful. God does not instigate the bad things that happen to people. Rather, terrible things happen to people because of their own or others' choices. God strengthens His children so that they can forge through and overcome the darkness. He also guides other people to help set wrongs right.

For Michelle, those individuals included Barbara, who became the mother Michelle never had; Dr. Natalie, her guiding healer; Ivan, her best friend; and Joy, an education mentor. The most important individuals were Michelle's children: Casey, who has amazing insight; Rachel, a medical doctor who always roots for the underdog and never wants anyone to be hurt; Naomi, a marine officer with a deep love for God and country; and Martha, who continually campaigns for the voices she feels deserve an audience.

Ivan was right. Michelle needed to unlock the next box. Its contents were the reason for her resistance. The contents needed to be brought into the light. But how? Even the thought of describing the contents of this next box brought Michelle to her knees.

"God," Michelle pleaded, "just this once let this box go. Please just let me keep this one hidden, and if not, then let me disappear when it is opened. Man, this is so hard. Harder than I ever thought it would be. I think the locks of this box are stronger than I am. Please, God, please let me get out of this. I thought I was strong, but this box will prove just how weak I was or maybe still am."

For the next several days Michelle picked up the phone on more than one occasion to cancel the next appointment with Dr. Natalie but never followed through. She had tasted healing, she had felt love, and in the core of her heart she knew she trusted Dr. Natalie and that somehow they would work through this. And if she was lucky, she would be okay—scarred and perhaps more broken, but okay.

CHAPTER 13

The Fifth Box: Healing Love

Silence is a meaningful part of healing. Many times, both client and therapist lack the understanding of silence's value and cast it aside, replacing it with constant chatter. Yet, in silence the heart can find the words necessary to heal a broken soul.

During the journey of healing, it's imperative to apply the balm of Gilead to the infected areas while elevating that which is untouched.

AT THE TIME OF MICHELLE'S NEXT APPOINTMENT, SHE SAT IN HER CAR, HAVING received a text message that Dr. Natalie was running a few minutes late. Michelle was grateful for a few more moments to contemplate the next box that she and Dr. Natalie would unlock. The last two days had been weighed down with mixed emotions—some identifiable, some more elusive. The predominant emotion was shame. Today, Dr. Natalie and Michelle would unlock a box that contained events in Michelle's adult life, with roots from the past.

When Dr. Natalie arrived, they both exited their vehicles and climbed the stairs to Dr. Natalie's office. Michelle selected a seat in the waiting room so that Dr. Natalie had time to prepare for their session. After a few minutes, Michelle heard the all-too-familiar statement, "Michelle, I'm ready."

"You might be, but I'm not sure I am," Michelle thought. Today, if this appointment proceeded as reasonable, Michelle would pull out the contents of a box she had pledged never to open, not even for Dr. Natalie. Michelle decided she wanted to stand instead of sit during this session, but standing seemed disrespectful, so Michelle sat at the end of the couch that was as far away from Dr. Natalie as possible.

"So, Michelle, how have the last two days gone for you?"

"The last few days have been grueling. On more than one occasion, I wanted to dial you and say, 'I am done' or 'Can I come in?' Obviously, I didn't act on either impulse, but I came close."

"So why didn't you?"

"Out of respect for your time and knowing I need this session to complete the healing process. I'm still not sure I'm ready for what we'll be discussing. I'm not sure one can prepare for the contents of the next box."

"So far, every box we've opened has been less damning than you thought it would be. Discussing these boxes has led to healing, light, and truth instead of darkness, hurt, and pain. That's important for you to remember as we start this session, particularly since you consider this next box to be potentially devastating to you as a person, how you view the world, and how others look at you.

"You know that I won't judge you. Nothing you've shared with me has tainted my perspective of you. If anything, learning more about you has elevated my insight about the human soul's amazing ability to thrive even when confronted by the depths of hell. Remember, I have years of experience helping individuals through darkness. After you empty this next box, its contents may not seem as horrible as you now consider them to be."

"Yes," Michelle thought, "you have experience on your side, but I have knowledge on mine. I'm aware of what's in the box, and you're not. Although I know you mean well, the contents of this box may alter your perspective."

"Dr. Natalie, I admit that as we've emptied boxes, my ability to trust, feel love, and recognize truth have increased. The medicine has been painful, but the benefits far exceed the side effects of the treatment. I'm different—in a positive way. Thank you. I feel like a weary traveler who bought a ticket to Japan but is now en route to Germany. I had no idea when we started this process that we'd arrive where we have. We could stop now, and this journey would have been worth it."

"Well, Michelle, I don't know where we've arrived at, but if I were that weary traveler, I'd be glad that I'd bought a ticket for Japan and ended up in Germany. I have always wanted to visit Germany."

Michelle smiled. "Okay, I stand corrected. We were headed to Japan but are now en route to Germany."

Silence returned to the room, and they let it take up residence for a while. The silence would help Michelle calm the arguments in her head and secure the key that would unlock the box.

"Dr. Natalie, I need to talk about an event that occurred several years ago. As a clinician, I believe that the contents of this box are attached to my past, but as the client I just believe I really crossed a line and that my actions had nothing to due with my past."

"Okay."

"You know that I'm a member of a religious faith whose doctrine contains strong moral directives."

"Yes, I am."

"I appreciate the fact that although we have different religious beliefs, you've respected mine during this process. What I'm about to share placed me in violation of a foundational doctrine of my faith."

"Okay."

"Here goes." Michelle's shame begged for increased physical and emotional distance from Dr. Natalie, so she moved to a corner of Dr. Natalie's office.

"About six years ago, I met . . . Okay, this is going to be as hard as I'd imagined."

"You met whom, Michelle? It's okay; we can talk about this."

"You don't even know what this is," Michelle thought.

"I met and . . . Oh my gosh. How can I say what I need to say? Not only is it inappropriate in my religion, but most of the world thinks it's wrong as well. I can't talk about this. Just forget I even brought it up. This box is staying locked, end of story." Michelle sat back down on the couch crossed her arms and legs and looked at the bookshelf across the room from Dr. Natalie. This session was over.

"Michelle, we can talk about this. I'm going to stay right here. You need to know that I may not share the same perspective as you regarding this subject." Michelle's eyes shifted from the bookshelf to Dr. Natalie. Dr. Natalie's words had not turned the key but had shattered the locks. Somehow Dr. Natalie knew.

"Michelle, I think it's time we talk about this. Don't you?"

"Sure." There was a long pause as Michelle attempted to gain composure and secure new locks to replace the ones Dr. Natalie had just shattered, to no avail. In a restricted voice Michelle started. "I met and formed a friendship with an individual who worked as an accountant in Alabama. We met at a conference and became quick friends. We had a lot in common and enjoyed being around each other. I do not know how to explain this, but for the first time in my life, I felt completely safe in her presence. It felt amazing. I felt like I always imagined a relationship should feel like."

"Relationship or friendship?" asked Dr. Natalie. Michelle halted as she bowed her head, tears forming in the corners of her eyes that represented both shame and lost love. Michelle knew to finish the telling she could not look at Dr. Natalie.

"Both. As our friendship progressed, I began to feel emotionally attracted to her. One evening, with no resistance on my part, we crossed a physical boundary. Before that, I didn't know that Robin was a lesbian, but that doesn't matter; I didn't resist.

"My head and my religious convictions said that what I was doing was wrong, but my heart disagreed. I felt loved in ways I can't explain. Even after ending the friendship and going through the repentance and confession process, I still had trouble conceptualizing that what we'd shared was wrong. I know what God teaches, and I know what society says. In ways I can't comprehend, that momentary relationship brought emotional and physical healing into my life. I was finally safe.

"I'm not trying to justify my actions. I'm just explaining how I felt. My head knows that what I did was wrong. I just wish my heart felt the same way. Now you know my dark secret. I willingly chose to do this; it wasn't done to me. I knew what Robin wanted that night, and I didn't stop her. How horrible is that! I am so tired of sexual issues being an encompassing part of my life."

Tears flowed freely as Michelle's heart and mind contended with each other.

"Michelle, can you look at me for a moment?" Michelle lifted her gaze, pleading for both acceptance and understanding, not judgment or condemnation. "I think you know that you and I are going to have to agree to disagree on this topic. Based on your past, I understand the reasons for your actions. The two of you were consenting adults. It's not my place to judge. I'm pleased that in my faith there is instruction to offer love and understanding instead of judgment. As a society, we're slowly moving in the right direction on the topic of same-gender attraction, and I think the younger generations are going to bring forth much-needed change.

"I think this topic would be less complicated for you to talk about if you felt in your heart that what you shared with Robin was inappropriate. You want to feel revolted, but you don't. You felt connected to Robin, and you felt safe in her embrace."

Dr. Natalie was right: if Michelle could get herself to feel horrible about what had transpired, the contents of this box wouldn't be as difficult to examine. Michelle had tried so long to make herself believe that what she had done with Robin was filthy and disgusting. But she had failed. Now to ask Dr. Natalie the hard question.

"Dr. Natalie, when we get to the end of this exploration, do you think I may uncover I have same-gender attraction?"

"You know, Michelle, I've asked myself that question a few times as we have talked. I'm not sure, but we might."

"We can't, Dr. Natalie. If I do have same-gender attraction, it'll destroy me and all I want to do with my life."

Michelle struggled to understand what the impact of same-gender attraction might have in her life. If she was a lesbian, she would have to choose between the religion she knew to be true and the gift of completing love. Since childhood, Michelle had sought complete love. She had found that completeness in Robin's touch. Even when Michelle was married, she did not find complete love. Michelle closed her eyes and thought, "Heavenly Father, isn't this enough? I ran from the sexual events of my childhood, and as an adult I've run into another one. I can't be attracted to women."

"Michelle let's set the same-gender issue aside and consider a few of the comments you made this evening as you shared the contents of this box. I think it's critical to explore some of these comments."

"Okay," Michelle said with doubt in her voice.

"I found it very intriguing when you used the words 'safe,' 'complete,' and 'connected' as you described the connection you shared with Robin. I didn't hear words like 'sexual,' 'erotic,' or 'physical.' Your word choices tell me that your relationship with Robin, although it had a physical component, was less about same-gender attraction and more about love, trust, and safety. In ways you may not yet understand, this relationship—not the sexual part—was part of your healing. You and I both know that healing comes in different ways and even in ways we would never imagine, such as your relationship with Robin."

As Michelle listened to Dr. Natalie's words, Michelle's heart agreed but her head argued. "That's a nice story, Dr. Natalie," Michelle noted in a slightly raised voice, "but you and I both know that in my faith and culture, no one is going to accept such a perspective. They are more likely to view it as an excuse."

"Perhaps, Michelle, but it doesn't matter what others think. What matters is the truth."

"That's easy for you to say; you're not a member of my faith. Do you realize that individuals can be removed from my faith for such acts?"

"Yes, I do, Michelle, and I've counseled many who were and some who were not. It would appear you have not been removed, which brings me to my next questions. Knowing how deep your faith is and aware of the personal relationship you have with your Heavenly Father, have you taken the repentance steps outlined by your faith regarding what you perceive to be an issue?"

Michelle was a little taken aback. She had not expected Dr. Natalie to ask about the repentance process, nor if she had partaken of such a gift. Silence sat in the office for what felt like an eternity with Dr. Natalie waiting for Michelle to speak. Michelle broke the silence.

"You know, Dr. Natalie, I did not see that question coming. I must admit you really caught me off guard this time. After all, we are not of the same faith, but I know you have in-depth knowledge of my beliefs. The answer to your question is yes. Yes, I followed the repentance steps of my faith."

"So, Michelle, if you have repented and if you believe in the atoning process, why are you still so self-condemning? Did it not work? Do you need to go back and do it again?"

Michelle again sat in silence for a long time, internalizing the fact that Dr. Natalie, in her own direct, yet kind way had reminded her of a truth she had forgotten and of the sacred journey she and her religious leader had taken many years ago. "Thank you, Dr. Natalie, I needed to be reminded of the true gift of repentance and the power of the Atonement. Thank you."

Dr. Natalie just smiled. She loved Michelle, and she knew God loved her as well.

"Michelle, why don't you tell me about your visit with your religious leader? I think that would be a great way to end our session tonight. Oh, but before you do, speaking of truth, I think in our next session it might be a good time to talk about your marriage."

"Oh, wow, I didn't see that coming, but okay?"

"Great, now tell me about your visit."

"Shortly after my encounters with Robin—yes, it happened more than once—I realized I could not stay in the relationship and be true to myself. I felt like I was being ripped in half. Robin on one side and my personal faith on the other. Now, when I say that, Dr. Natalie, I am not referring to a religion. I am referring to my understandings and connection with God. I know that others' faith and connection with God is not the same as mine, and I am glad we are starting to recognize such beautiful relationships and support those who have same-gender attraction and are in same-gender marriages. To stop my internal battle and to bring my soul closer to peace, I ended the friendship. Ending that friendship was one of the hardest decisions I have ever made in my adult life. I walked away from love. At first, after the friendship ended, I told myself that I did not need to repent. That what Robin and I shared was different. That it was a way for me to feel safe and to heal. Yet deep in my heart of hearts I knew the steps of repentance would return full peace to my life.

"So, after much prayer, scripture study, and fasting I made an appointment to meet with the religious leader of the congregation I belonged to. After making the appointment my whole life turned upside down. I could not sleep; I could not eat. I think I had a few major panic attacks. I was so scared of what could happen that I didn't trust God and just let it happen. My faith means everything to me, and the thought of losing it was almost incomprehensible."

"Michelle, were you at risk of losing your faith, or your membership in a church? Are they different or the same thing?"

"That is a great question. Thank you. No, I was not at risk of losing my faith, but a membership in a church. But at the time I did not separate the two. I do now."

"Did you call Ivan for support? I can't even begin to imagine how hard this must have been for you."

"No, I told no one. I did not want anyone to know. I was so humiliated and devastated and my pride held strong. How did I let myself make such a horrific mistake?"

"Was it a mistake?"

"No, it was indeed a learning experience, and believe it or not my meeting with my religious leaders helped me understand that in ways only the repentance process could allow."

"How so?"

"I knew the church policies on same-sex attraction, and I knew I could lose everything that I thought mattered to me, yet as I made the phone call, set the date to meet with my religious leader, and prepared for the meeting, my faith, not the church, taught me that what I feared losing was man's outward recognition versus my inward relationship with God.

"It didn't matter if I was removed from the membership of a church. What mattered more was that I was right in my eyes before God."

"Very insightful. Although I still do not believe as you do, I am glad to see your feeling and thoughts shifted."

"Thank you. When the night of my appointment arrived, I entered the office of my religious leader at peace. I knew I would tell them all that needed to be told. I knew that they were not my judge and that this was just a process. My only judge and the only person I truly had to answer to, who knew my heart and my full life story, was my Savior Jesus Christ."

"So, what happened?"

"I started to tell them my story to explain what happen. About one minute into my explanation my religious leader stopped me and said, 'Michelle, you do not need to tell me any more. Your Heavenly Father loves you so much and He has said it is enough. Thank you for coming to see me all is forgiven, and the church will take no action.'"

"Wow, I have never ever heard of your religion handling the reason you went to talk in such a way. God loves you a lot. He really knows who you are,

Michelle, and you believe in Him. In your childhood it is clear you developed a very strong foundation of love and trust in God."

"Yes, Dr. Natalie, I know He loves me, and He is the reason I am who I am today."

"Yes, Michelle, I believe He and your Auntie Vi are the reasons you are who you are, but you are who you are also because you have repeatedly made the decision to survive and to make life a better place for others."

"Thank you, Dr. Natalie. Thank you for hearing me and for not judging me. But more than that, thank you for loving me."

"You're welcome, Michelle. Thank you for trusting me. I'm so sorry you went through that alone. That must have been so hard."

"Yes, it was, but it was worth it, and tonight has reminded me to re-find the peace I felt the night I left my religious leader's office and to hold on to it always."

As Dr. Natalie and Michelle parted that night, Michelle recognized that her admiration for Dr. Natalie had deepened. Michelle also recognized that her acceptance of and love for herself had increased through the powerful and sacred gift of therapy founded in truth and sustained by the Atonement of Jesus Christ. As Michelle drove home that night, tranquility filled her car, along with a little confusion as to why Dr. Natalie wanted to talk about her former marriage.

A smile formed on Michelle's lips as she gazed at the Curious George stuffed animal that adorned her dashboard. Michelle had told Dr. Natalie in one of their sessions that during her childhood, Curious George had reminded Michelle that nothing could get her down unless she let it.

Several weeks after the Curious George conversation, Dr. Natalie had presented Michelle with a small Curious George as a reminder that nothing had kept Michelle down. Tonight, Michelle discerned that truth at a finite level. In Michelle's life, she had experienced many Mount Moriahs, and each required sacrifice with both negative and positive facets. In tonight's session, as in so many previous sessions, Dr. Natalie helped Michelle to see the good qualities she had developed because of her childhood. Michelle's childhood had held darkness, which Michelle now no longer tried to hide, and it had also held great light—light far more intense than the darkness. Michelle, with Dr. Natalie's careful stewardship, worked to remove darkness while safeguarding truth.

When Dr. Natalie and Michelle arrived at the end of their therapy journey, Michelle determined that she didn't have same-gender attraction. Michelle's healing journey allowed her to let go of negative sexual concepts while embracing truth regarding her sexual desires. As the darkness left Michelle's life, light entered and allowed her to understand why the sexual encounter with Robin happened and to understand her sexual orientation. Michelle also reached the understanding that if she did have same-gender attraction, then that would be okay, and such would also be okay within her faith. God loves each of us for who we are while encouraging each of us to find His path for us within His gospel plan.

Sadly, we live in a world that's far too quick to judge instead of investing time to understand people. God should be the only judge. Love and understanding are needed, but many people selfishly withhold these attributes because of pride and fear. Judgments would be different if we each truly took the time to know each other's back story as Michelle and Natalie did. Knowing the back story and face to face connection are a major reason therapy can be so effective.

Michelle understands that one can love and support and care for those who live or love contrary to her beliefs. Showing love doesn't mean Michelle compromised her beliefs; rather, it means that she manifested her beliefs at a deeper level. If Michelle was given the chance to go back and not become involved with Robin, she would not take it. That relationship taught Michelle many priceless lessons.

Michelle longed for even more light, so she decided that before her therapy sessions ended, she would leave all the darkness behind. Michelle wanted to empty all the boxes, even the ones she thought no one would ever know about. Having made this decision, Michelle said to Curious George, "There are three more boxes. Then, my friend, this life-altering journey can come to a close."

Michelle was at peace. She knew all the unlocking was worth it and that both she and Dr. Natalie were changing.

CHAPTER 14

The Sixth Box:
The End of a Marriage

In life, people make sacred marriage covenants that are intended to last forever. Individuals should enter these relationships with full purpose of heart and work toward maintaining them. When the marital relationship makes both individuals better, creates union, and fosters peace and joy, this relationship should be celebrated and preserved. When the relationship creates discord, disharmony, and emotional harm, then the union no longer serves its eternal purpose and needs to be altered or ended.

WHEN MICHELLE ARRIVED FOR HER NEXT THERAPY SESSION, SHE WASN'T quite sure what to think or feel. Dr. Natalie had indicated she wanted this session to focus on Michelle's former marriage to Devin Redland. Michelle had no idea why—Devin wasn't part of her childhood abuse. At least, that's what Michelle thought as she entered Dr. Natalie's office, chose a seat on her couch, and waited for her to explain why she wanted to talk about Michelle's former marriage.

"Michelle, how are you feeling after our last session?"

"I feel great, like a thousand pounds has been lifted from my shoulders. That last session was heavy but liberating for my soul."

"That's good. As boxes empty, there is room for healing. So where should we begin today?"

"You indicated you wanted to talk about my former marriage. I'm not sure why, so perhaps you can enlighten me."

"Michelle, as we've taken this journey, you've mentioned your marriage in passing, but have said very little about why the marriage ended or how that affected you. Marriage is such an important part of your faith. I also know that in your faith, deciding to divorce is very difficult and often heart-wrenching. When I think about that, it seems a little odd that it's something we've never discussed . . . and I wonder if it's something we should talk about."

Michelle sat in silence for a few minutes. Dr. Natalie was correct: in Michelle's religion, deciding to get divorced is complex because marriage is considered to be a potentially eternal union. Michelle's faith also strongly believes that children should be blessed with having both biological parents in the home.

Breaking her silence, Michelle noted, "Wow, this is one topic I was not planning on addressing, and I'm not sure where to begin or how to explain my marital journey. Although the reasons for the divorce transpired over years, the divorce was handled respectfully. Even today, Devin and I maintain respectful, limited interaction. As two highly educated individuals, we understood that how we processed our divorce would directly affect the emotional stability of our children.

"Our children were not the reason for the divorce, so we made sure, at least to the best that two people can, that our children were not victims of the divorce. At no time did Devin or I speak poorly of one another to our children. If at any time the children were not acting as I thought they should, I called Devin, and he would talk to them and encourage them to be respectful to their mother. If privileges were restricted at my home, they were also restricted at Devin's home. Devin was included in all the major family events and was welcome to be with the kids whenever accommodations could be made. I wish he'd decided to be more involved in his kids' lives after the marriage ended, but that's his issue, not mine. Devin and I made sure our children never felt like they had to choose sides."

"That's great. So many parents could avoid a lot of damage that's done to children in the divorce process. Divorce affects kids, but kids are resilient and if the divorce is processed in a mature healthy manner, kids can thrive. I think it's actually better for kids to be with two parents who are happy in separate homes than to be in a home that's filled with fighting, anger, hatred, and chaos."

"I agree with that."

"So now, Michelle, I know how you processed the divorce, but I don't know why you divorced or how the divorce affected you personally. I'd like to know why and how."

"Oh boy. I wasn't really thinking about this box prior to your comments last session, and now here it is in the middle of your office. I guess I thought that my marriage had not contributed to the journey we're on, but now I'm beginning to wonder if the marriage did. As a psychologist, I understand that oftentimes a person who grows up in an abusive situation may end up selecting a person with traits similar to the abusers, due to trauma bonding issues. I am fairly certain that I did not marry Devin for that reason. He wasn't physically abusive.

"I can tell you that for several years after my divorce, due to my personal expectations for life and my personal perspectives, I felt like a failure. You know, it's interesting that my faith teaches that divorce isn't a sin but when it happens, it sure feels like you sinned. After my divorce, I was not invited to serve in my faith for over two years. Not a single church leader came to my home to inquire about how I was doing. Because I didn't feel worthy, it took all I had to go to church each Sunday. I needed to serve. I needed to be needed—I so desperately needed someone to ask me if I was okay. Someone to notice me. But I was that strong, independent female who I'm sure everyone believed had it all together. Yet I had never felt so broken. For months, I pleaded for a hand to reach out and extend love, but it never came. Now, as I look back, I know I should have reached out and asked, but my pride was in the way. I loved my Heavenly Father. I knew His teachings, and I never wanted to break up a family.

"Do you have any idea how hard it is to go from sitting with your family during services to sitting alone? On so many Sundays, I just wished someone would invite me to sit with them, but it never happened. And to make matters worse, I was the only divorced female in the congregation. I was no longer invited to activities with other couples; there were no invitations to backyard barbeques. Friends not of my faith treated me the same as before, but not the people of my faith. I guess they weren't sure what to do with me. I wasn't sure how to feel either.

"In many ways, I felt like I had this big *D* on my shirt. I can tell you this: if my faith was not founded on the teachings of Jesus Christ, I would've walked away from my church, never to return. I'm so grateful I didn't, but I know many divorced members of the church who feel or felt the same way I did and who have walked away.

"Eventually, I realized that I needed to change my perspective. Although it took a few months, I came to realize in a spiritual way that I had not failed. Rather, life had just shifted, and in that shifting I could find truth and understanding."

"Michelle, I'm sorry about the pain you went through. Divorce isn't an easy process, and one's faith can make divorce even more complex."

"Yes, I definitely agree."

"So, from your perspective, what caused the divorce? You noted that Devin wasn't physically abusive. Was he emotionally or sexually abusive?"

"I'm not quite sure how to answer that question. I think Devin would tell you no, and I'm not sure I would say yes, but I can tell you that we had very different perspectives regarding sexual activities, and on more than one occasion 'no' was not acceptable because I was his wife and sex was his right."

"Michelle, I think that is called rape."

"Yeah, I know, but I have never quite looked at it that way."

"Why not? I am positive you, Dr. Chambers, would tell a client it was rape."

"Yes, but I was broken."

"Is that you talking or Devin?"

"I think I need to explain."

"Okay, I'm listening."

"Shortly after Devin and I were married, he started to request certain sexual acts in the bedroom that I wasn't comfortable with. I explained my reasons, which Devin acknowledged verbally but ultimately ignored. And because I'd told him about some of my childhood experiences, he'd use the information against me, claiming if they hadn't happened, I'd have no issue performing sexually in my marriage. When I gave in and did what Devin demanded, he was easy to get along with. When I denied him, he at times backed down. However, he became angrier in everyday life. Six months into our marriage I packed my bags to leave. Devin stopped me and promised he would change, and he would stop forcing me to do certain sexual acts. I believed him and stayed. Shortly after my decision to stay I found out I was pregnant with our first child. The expected birth made it even more complicated to leave, and so I stayed for years, vacillating between doing what Devin demanded to keep his anger at bay and not giving in and dealing with his anger. The hard part was that as our kids aged Devin's anger was not only aimed at me but also at the kids. I found it easier to give in and do what he requested sexually rather than deal with his anger. I had to try to protect my kids.

"On more than one occasion, I asked Devin if we could visit with a counselor or talk to our religious leader. Devin made it clear that if I ever told anyone about our bedroom issues, he'd divorce me. I believed him.

"Both Devin and I were serving in our church. We were both highly educated and had married later in life. It appeared as if we had everything going for us. So, for years I did what he required. Then after about sixteen years of marriage I just couldn't continue doing what he asked. I can't really explain why. It's like something just broke.

"Shortly afterward, Devin left on a business trip, I made an appointment to meet with our religious leader. In the meeting, I explained the bedroom issues Devin and I were having. After listening to my concerns, this leader claimed he found it hard to believe both that Devin was capable of such demands and that

Devin had a temper—this leader viewed me as the dominant individual in the marriage. Unfortunately, he perceived that my education, my career, my public leadership roles, and my effective articulation abilities were negative rather than positive. This leader informed me that before he offered any counsel or direction, he wanted to visit with Devin when he got home. This leader also told me to refrain from any sexual activity with Devin until after the two of them spoke. This request made me very concerned. I knew that when Devin arrived home, the first item on his agenda would be sex and that when I told him our religious leader wanted to talk to Devin, he would be quite upset.

"When Devin arrived home, he requested sex and I informed him that I had visited with our religious leader regarding the bedroom issues I felt uncomfortable about. Devin again said that it was not anyone's business what happened in our bedroom and that he would divorce me if I didn't satisfy his sexual needs and if I talked with our religious leader again about the situation.

"I couldn't do what Devin demanded sexually, even though I tried. I truly tried because I knew that if I could just do what he wanted, then I could keep my marriage. But I could not do what he demanded. After several years of my trying to meet Devin's needs, we divorced. If you asked Devin why we divorced he will tell you it was because I was emotionally unavailable. That I was more connected to our children and to friends than to him, and Devin would be right. After repeatedly being raped in my marriage and forced to perform certain sexual acts I emotionally detached. I went through the motions but without feelings."

"You know, Michelle, that your emotional detachment allowed you to survive the marriage as long as you did."

"Yes, Dr. Natalie, I understand that, but that emotional detachment impacted all aspects of mine and Devin's relationship, not just the bedroom."

"Yes, I am sure it did."

"I wanted to be any place but with Devin, so I started to pack my evenings as full as I could get them with activities for my kids and meetings for me. I did all that I could to make sure I was not at home with him. I now know my being gone all the time and not addressing our marital issue sooner led to many of Devin's frustrations, and I think in some ways his forcefulness in the bedroom. I am not justifying what Devin did, but I do know the marriage ending was also partly my issues as well."

"You know, Michelle, in most marriages it takes two to make it, and it takes two to break it, but there are cases when it is weighted more on one side of the aisle than the other. In your case, I think more weight rests with Devin than you."

"Yes, perhaps that is the case, but I am not his judge. I can only answer for my own mistakes and mishaps."

"Yes, indeed that is all any of us can do."

"Dr. Natalie, there was one night, shortly after Devin and I had met with our religious leader and started marriage counseling, that I did everything Devin wanted. I wore the sexy lingerie. I initiated the sexual acts he preferred and for several hours allowed him to watch what he wanted to watch in a sexual genre, and then I acted out what he watched. I did it all. When Devin was what I considered satisfied we went to sleep. About two hours later I woke up to offer him more sex, and to my surprise Devin was not in the bedroom. I started to look all over the house for him. Believe it or not, I found him upstairs in our daughters' bathroom in the shower masturbating. Devin did not know I found him. I left the bathroom unnoticed and went back to bed. That night, Dr. Natalie, I realized I would never be able to satisfy Devin's sexual needs. I cannot explain it, but that night as I walked back down the stairs something broke and I knew I was done. I had nothing left to give."

"That must have been so hard to find him that way. Did you ever tell him?"

"No."

"Did you tell your marriage counselor?"

"No."

"Why not?"

"I guess at that point I knew I was done and figured it didn't matter."

"Wow, thank you for sharing. I cannot image how hard that was."

"To this day, there is a part of me that wishes I could've done what Devin wanted. I know my kids didn't want to have divorced parents, and I know that when I married Devin, I intended the marriage to last forever."

"It's interesting that even in your marriage, you experienced sexual abuse."

"You know, I never thought of it quite that way, but I think you're right. For a long time, I just thought there was something wrong with me. On more than one occasion, Devin would tell me that what he wanted in the bedroom was normal and that if I truly loved him, I'd do what he needed. I guess I believed him, and maybe I still do."

"What do you mean, 'Maybe I still do'?"

"If I'd been able to keep doing what he wanted, then I wouldn't be divorced, and my kids would have both of their parents in their lives more often. Devin remarried, and she and her kids take priority, with our kids coming in second. I make sure they are always first in my life, but I know it hurts them that Devin is more interested in his current wife and her kids.

"My son has chosen to distance himself from Devin, mostly based on the anger my son saw as a child. On more than one occasion, if I wasn't meeting

Devin's demands in the bedroom, he broke things, like chairs and cupboard doors, and the kids saw.

"I'm blessed to have a great relationship with all my kids. They know they can come to me for anything and that if I can help them, I will. They are moving forward with their lives and no longer really seek a relationship with their father. They care about him, but I'm the one they share their hopes and dreams with. I have no regrets when it comes to my kids. I know that my kids are half me and half Devin. Now that you and I are on this journey, I do wonder whether things between Devin and me might have been different if I'd broken my silence during our first year of marriage or if I had started counseling sooner. I guess we'll never know."

"How do you feel now about your divorce?"

"Most of the time I feel like I made the right decision, but there are moments that I wonder. Divorce is never easy, regardless of why it happens."

"Yes, I can understand that. Thank you for telling me what happened. I'm glad you feel that you've processed the feelings and emotions around your marital abuse. But I'm not so sure that you truly have."

"I want to be healed from the marital damage." Michelle's voice started to crack. "My marriage to Devin made me question a lot about myself and my personal sexuality."

"What do you mean?"

"For years Devin told me over and over again that it was my fault our sex life didn't work, that if I'd been a real woman, I'd have known how to please her man. It's hard at times to get those words out of my head. They make me question if I could remarry. I'd like to marry again, but maybe I'm broken. So here we go again."

"What do you mean, 'Here we go again'?"

"Dealing with another part of my life clouded by sexual abuse. Can't we just get away from this?"

"I think we are as we open each box, empty its contents, and throw away the key."

"Agreed. I just want it to go faster."

"So, Michelle, what do we need to work on regarding this box?"

"I need to talk about the sexual abuse that happened in my marriage, my feelings regarding the abuse while allowing blame to stand at the door, where it belongs. I need to realize that the abuse doesn't mean marriage is out of the question."

"Agreed."

For the next several hours Dr. Natalie and Michelle processed the sexual abuse and rapes Michelle experienced during her marriage and Michelle's feelings about it. As they talked, Michelle was able to let go of self-blame and allowed herself to create her personal boundaries regarding intimacy.

CHAPTER 15
Personal Faith Examination

In the field of psychology, there are multiple studies regarding spirituality and the healing process. Research indicates that individuals who hold to their own belief system and believe life has a purpose progress through therapy faster and achieve deeper, longer-lasting feelings of peace and contentment than do other individuals who do not see a purpose to life and lack a personal belief system.

As MICHELLE ARRIVED FOR HER NEXT SESSION, SHE KNEW THAT SHE AND DR. Natalie wouldn't focus on unlocking a certain box that night. Instead, they would review spiritual questions that had arisen during their journey.

After they greeted each other, Michelle introduced the direction of their session by explaining, "Dr. Natalie, this journey has given me time to examine both the past and the present and to consider and discover truth. Today, I'd like to talk about some of those discoveries."

"I think that's a great topic, Michelle. Healing allows us to explore all aspects of our lives. I think as we deal with events of the past, we can look at our present more honestly."

Michelle agreed. As Michelle resolved issues regarding her past, she had discovered that portions of her religion's doctrine were more difficult to accept.

"Dr. Natalie, since my baptism and conversion to my religion during my teenage years, I've followed its doctrine without many questions. Now, as my heart heals and boxes empty, I'm grateful that many of my core values continue to align with the doctrine. However, I also acknowledge a rising conflict between certain personal values and teachings of this organization."

"I wondered if and when we might have this conversation. Thank you for opening this discussion. Before we proceed, I want to reiterate that I respect your faith and will help you to decide the direction you want to take, but I want to be careful not to influence you in that process. You must decide your direction, for this will affect your life and needs to reflect your spiritual truth."

"Yes, it's my decision to examine this topic in our session. I'm bringing up this topic based on deep reflection. Over the past several years my understandings of my faith's doctrine has increased, leading to matured spirituality. My spirituality has a critical influence on the way I live my life, how I treat others, and the decisions I make. I also know that my belief in God was a major reason I survived my childhood. I don't question my belief in Heavenly Father and the Savior Jesus Christ, but I struggle with my perception of the requirement that spirituality be manifested in the form of an organized religion."

"Michelle, in your mind is there a difference between your faith and organized religion, or are they one and the same?"

"I believe in individualized spiritually that's guided and directed by faith-based teaching. I've observed many people who make the organization their faith rather than making their spiritual understanding their faith."

"I also see a difference between spirituality and religion, Michelle. So, if you know your spirituality is based in God and Jesus Christ and not in an organization, then what's creating the conflict? Can you belong to a religion while maintaining your own spirituality?"

"Yes, I think so. What's causing my unrest is certain teachings within my religion that, at this time, feel contrary to my core values."

"Can you give me some examples?"

"Yes, I can. Examples include how women are perceived, the role of society, and how same-gender attraction is viewed. As you know, many of my very good friends are gay. They are some of the greatest individuals I know. They love God and seek each day to be a positive influence in others' lives. They are members of my faith, and some of them a have always stayed faithful, while others have chosen a different path. How can their desires to love another of their same gender be wrong? How can one be asked to live their life alone, forever denying themselves human intimate contact?"

"That's a good question, Michelle, and is a reason to give you pause as you consider what you want in your life moving forward."

"It's so not easy to resolve this question and others. I can't deny what I know is true and I don't want to leave my faith, but how do I resolve the conflict I feel? I know that true faith allows for receiving spiritual direction, setting aside what we may not understand fully, and trusting that in due time we will understand all things.

"I'm not seeking immediate answers, but my soul needs to resolve the conflict I feel. For far too long, I've lived in incongruency, running from my childhood and blaming myself for the actions of others. Today, my past and present are more congruent. I feel peace and understanding that I lack words to express. I don't want splinters in my life. I need to find peace spiritually, and I desire to find that peace within the faith I know to be true."

"Thank you for your openness and honesty. You are a person of great faith, and that's been your sustaining power in overcoming darkness. I know that whether or not you decide to stay in the religion you belong to, your faith will stand. In my own life, I've taken such a journey. The journey was not easy, but it led me to live with centered spirituality instead of outward observation and guilt. How can I help you in your own process?"

"You know, I'm not sure. I do know that giving voice to my concerns is helpful. I can't share these feelings with others for two main reasons—either I'll be told to leave and never look back, or I'll be asked why I'm losing my faith. What should I be doing to get it back? I feel closer to my Heavenly Father right now than ever before. I think that previously, I kept a barricade between us. I know that Christ tutored His followers to seek truth, and that's my quest today."

"I know that you won't rest until you find answers. Again, Michelle, remember that you are not in a race. As you noted, in due time all truth will come into the light. Darkness can't withstand the light."

"No, it can't, and truth is discovered when the seeker is humbly willing to accept it. Thank you for allowing me to be vulnerable."

"You're welcome."

"I am glad that this session was a little lighter than the others we've had. I know we still have a few more boxes, and I know we'll get to them. But for right now, I appreciate a lighter session, knowing next week will likely be weighty."

"Speaking of our next session, I'll be out of town for the next three weeks, and I think we're in a good place to allow some time between sessions. How do you feel about that?"

"You know, if you'd asked in an earlier session, I might have freaked out, but I agree we're in a good place and can take some time before our next session."

"Great. I'll see you when I get back."

As Michelle left Dr. Natalie's office that night, she hesitated to make her usual call to Ivan. Ivan had his own crosses to carry. As Michelle contemplated whether to call, a resounding answer came: you know that Ivan will love you no matter what choice you make. He may not approve, but that won't change the love he has for you.

Michelle dialed his number, and after he answered they chatted about various topics, including Michelle's current spiritual crusade.

"So how did it go with Dr. Natalie?"

"You know, Ivan, tonight's session was lighter. It was nice and not so emotionally draining. It was more of a chance for me just to explore a few of my thoughts with a trusted advisor who would not offer what I will refer to as patent church answers."

"Sounds interesting. What topic did you want advice on?"

Michelle paused. She knew how much Ivan loved his faith and how committed he was to all of its teachings. "Well, tonight, Ivan, we talked about the church and certain issues I have with some of the things it teaches."

"Oh, wow, I didn't know you had concerns. Considering Dr. Natalie is not of our faith, why did you talk to her?"

"Because I knew she would listen without judging or trying to sway me one way or the other. I knew she would be truly neutral and would just let me talk."

"That makes sense. So what are you thinking now about the church? I mean, like, what are your concerns?"

"You know, Ivan, if it is okay with you, I'd like to leave that conversation just between me and Dr. Natalie."

"Okay, I can respect that."

"Thank you. I love you, my friend."

"Love you too."

At the close of their conversation, Ivan affirmed, "I know you, and I know you'll stay in the faith you hold. You may question and you may even try to run, but you love God so much that you'll always do what you know to be right. So, question all you want. Seek for all the answers you want. I'm not worried, because I know you and so does God. Not only does He know you, but He also loves you and trusts you, and that's what matters. Oh, and you trust Him. So, sleep well, my friend. You're safe."

Ivan was right. Michelle would seek. She would ponder, and she would stay. Michelle stayed because she knew truth, and she knew God's love. Michelle knew this life isn't full of perfection; rather, it's full of mortals striving to do the best they can. Michelle wouldn't find answers to all her questions, but she would have answers, and that would be enough. Each day, Michelle continued to learn and receive greater light. It would be okay to still need some answers. What Michelle knew would have a far greater effect than what she didn't know. She wasn't seeking perfection. She was seeking truth within the religion she belonged to, and in Michelle's personal spirituality she would find truth.

CHAPTER 16

The Seventh Box: Personal Acceptance

One major difference between emotional mending and physical mending is that the treatment for emotional healing varies from person to person. When someone breaks a bone, the standard treatment involves setting the bone and putting a cast on it. In cases of emotional injury, one or more treatment modalities can be applied and tailored to the individual's clinical needs. It's ineffective to compare one person's emotional trauma to that of another person. When a client or a therapist compares the client with someone else, the power of healing is shackled.

THROUGHOUT THE THREE WEEKS THAT DR. NATALIE WAS OUT OF TOWN, the boxes that remained unopened increased in weight and significance as Michelle reviewed them. The contents of these boxes, just as with the last one, were connected to the past and the present. Some people might have thought that the contents of these boxes were far less significant than what was in the boxes Michelle had already opened, but she didn't think so. Michelle also realized the weight of these boxes only warranted the consideration of Dr. Natalie and her, as therapy is truly a confidential journey. Michelle did not need to tell anyone else.

Toward the end of the second week, Michelle sent Dr. Natalie a text message indicating that there was another box they needed to unlock and that it would perhaps be the hardest box of all to open. Part of Michelle wanted to open the box, and part of her did not. Several hours later, Dr. Natalie replied, letting Michelle know that she had suspected there was another box and that she would like to see her on Monday, the day after she returned to town. Dr. Natalie also proposed that if the boxes became too heavy, while she was gone, Michelle could spend some time painting what was in the box. Art therapy, if effectively practiced, can allow a client to put on canvas what they might have a hard time talking about, emotionally releasing, or understanding. Michelle found the suggestion to paint interesting. She had encouraged her own clients to do the same but had never considered that as an option for her own therapy.

Scheduling the appointment calmed Michelle's soul, which wanted the release that would accompany the unlocking process. But her pride and ego feared what such unbolting might mean. Perhaps painting on canvas would help lift her fear and allow her to find more peace while Michelle waited for Dr. Natalie's return.

Michelle went to a local craft store and purchased the necessary items to paint. At first Michelle just sat in front of the canvas and wondered what to paint. Her mind and soul felt dark and tormented—almost as if she were in a cave she could not escape. A cave that contained personal and religious condemnation.

"That's what I will paint," Michelle said in an audible voice. "I will paint the darkness of a cave." Soon, amidst brush strokes, color blending, and swirling black, Michelle's soul painted a black hole that revealed the swirling cosmic clouded sky above with a child looking up through the darkness. As Michelle stepped back from the canvas and reviewed her work, tears flooded forward. In a loud voice that only she could hear Michelle cried, "Why, God, why can't this just be over with? Why can't we just be done? Why, God, over and over, is it sexual violations that haunt my life? Have I not paid a deep enough price? When will I ever be clean? When, God, when will this ever be over? Please, God. *When?* This process with Dr. Natalie is taking so long, and I just want it over. I can't—I just can't talk about this next box."

The night before their appointment, Michelle didn't sleep well. The box was in clear view shadowed by the painting, but Michelle wasn't sure how she would explain this box to Dr. Natalie. Perhaps she would begin with showing her the painting. Michelle didn't know exactly why the box's contents caused such darkness.

The next day, Michelle arrived at Dr. Natalie's office just before 9:00 a.m. with the painting in hand. Michelle stayed in her car until the last second; staying there felt emotionally safer than waiting in the reception area. As Michelle approached the door to Dr. Natalie's office, Dr. Natalie invited her to enter. Michelle claimed a seat on one end of the couch and kept her sunglasses on.

Dr. Natalie stood and dimmed the lights and broke the silence with the caring question, "How are you?"

Not wanting to answer her question, Michelle said, "I have something I need to tell you; I just don't know how."

With kindness in her voice, Dr. Natalie noted, "It's okay, Michelle. I think I know what's in the box, and together we can empty it. How about we start with what you brought into my office?"

"Yeah, okay. I can do that." Michelle unwrapped the canvas and turned it toward Dr. Natalie.

"That is an interesting painting. Can you tell me about it?"

"Well, when you suggested I paint this box, this is what I came up with. It is a cave with a girl stuck in the bottom of all this darkness looking up at the sky with no idea how to get out."

"Very interesting. I see the cave, I see the sky, but I could not tell if the person, which I knew was you, was looking into the cave or out of the cave."

"Wow. I can see why you are questioning that."

"Maybe, Michelle, after we finish this next box you might see yourself looking into the cave instead of looking out of it."

"Perhaps. I know that has been the case of a few of our sessions."

"How did you feel as you painted this?"

"I felt both angry and deeply sad. I am getting so tired of this process. I keep thinking we're done, but then no—there is one more box. How much more can there be? I'm just so ready to finish. I figured this would only take a few months, and here we are over a year later working on all the crap I left alone so long ago. I just want it over."

"I can understand that. I want it over too, but I want it over knowing you won't be coming back and that you will be at peace."

"Yeah, I want that too. Guess it's time to tell you about the next box." Michelle sat quietly for a long time, looking at the picture she had painted and seeking to find the strength to pull from its clutches the content of the next box.

"Dr. Natalie, I've worked so hard to bury this box. The contents of this box started in my childhood and continued after the physical and sexual abuse ended. During my teenage years, the box continually reminded me of my unworthiness and brokenness. You know, I'm not sure I can talk about this. I'm not sure if this box will make any sense. In the psychology world, many would say that what I'm struggling to disclose is a normal part of development and a normal part of life. For me, that's not the case. For me, it created a hazardous roller coaster."

"Michelle, you're safe, and we can unlatch this box together. Take your time—you're my only appointment this morning."

"I don't think any amount of time will allow me to heal from the contents of this box." As tears again flowed, Michelle decided that standing in the corner of Dr. Natalie's office was a much better location than the couch for the confession she was going to make.

"Dr. Natalie, it felt like every day of my childhood was saturated with sexual content. When I allow myself to wander through what should have been my years of innocence, I see that they are littered with sexual impurity. My childhood was contaminated, reminding me on a daily basis that I was bad. Today, I need to bring to light an aspect of sexual misconduct that wasn't perpetrated by someone else but that I instigated."

Silence returned to the office, and tears flowed down Michelle's cheeks. Michelle could not say what she knew needed to be said. This box didn't contain condemnation of others; it contained condemnation of herself. In her mind, the box's contents made Michelle no better than the abusers of her past.

"Michelle, I have a good idea what you need to say. As I told you on the phone, because of my experience with many individuals who are of your same faith, I think I have known for a long time, but I knew you needed time to be ready to open this box. I also know that this box is damning in your mind because of the faith you hold near to your heart. As with the contents of a previous box, we might have to agree to disagree on whether you're at fault."

Slowly, Michelle removed her sunglasses and, through tears, looked at Dr. Natalie. Dr. Natalie knew the secret in Michelle's box, but Dr. Natalie hadn't given it voice because she understood that Michelle needed the catharsis that would result from her confessing the stain.

"Michelle, you can tell me. I know you can give this box a voice, and we'll work through this box just as we have the ones in the past."

Michelle didn't want to say the words. These words sounded and felt disgusting in the chambers of her heart, and Michelle knew the same would be true if she spoke the words.

"Dr. Natalie, when I felt lost, alone, or stressed as a child, I would at time . . . Nope. I'm not going to say this. It will prove that I'm no better than the ones who created the boxes you and I have opened. I can't do this."

"Yes, you can. You are so close."

In a voice muffled by tears and shame, Michelle surrendered the words. "I would masturbate." Having confessed, Michelle felt engulfed in shame. She didn't feel relief. This session was over. Michelle quickly turned, preparing to leave the office. Michelle had just proven how horrible of a person she was, and she needed space.

"Michelle, can you give me a just few moments? Then you can leave."

Only Michelle's respect for Dr. Natalie stopped her from leaving. "Dr. Natalie, nothing you say can change how I view myself. Can you even image how hard it was as a teenager to sit through religious meetings on morality and know you were breaking God's laws? I lived in fear that someone would find out. I tried so many times to stop, and finally, after leaving home, I broke through and left the behavior behind me. What makes it so damning is that I did it over and over again, even though I knew it was wrong. I can't explain why, and I hate myself for it. This session is done!"

"Michelle, does the Atonement of Jesus Christ apply to you?"

Michelle stopped moving toward the door. "In general, it does, but not in this case. I knew it was wrong."

"Dr. Chambers, what would you say if a client disclosed this information to you?"

"That's so not fair."

"Oh, I think it is. Would you tell them they were evil, guilty, or unclean?"

"No, I would not, but I'm not them. I knew better."

"So, what would you tell them?" In a slightly sharp tone, Michelle said, "I'd tell them that such actions were a normal response to their childhood. I'd tell them that they had been prematurely sexualized, which had disrupted boundaries while imprinting sexual release as a form of self-soothing. But that doesn't apply to me. What I did was disgusting and wrong."

"Again, I have a different perspective of masturbation, so we're going to have to disagree there, but I'll agree with your clinical assessment. You were a child who was forced to survive horrible events, a child who didn't know love and appropriate touch. Every typical aspect of childhood was distorted. It's clear how powerful of an individual you are in that you didn't carry the negative aspects of your childhood into the lives of your kids. Your kids have no idea how lucky they are.

"Michelle, you did nothing wrong. I'm so sorry you've carried this guilt for so long. God loves you. He always has. You need to forgive little Michelle and let go of this shame. This shame is a major cause of the distance that remains between you and others."

Michelle's tears intensified. Each drop helped her broken soul to heal. Finally, Michelle said what needed to be said. She had released the truth from one of her darkest boxes. As Michelle's pride yielded to truth, she felt the shackles on her soul release and her ascent from the cave begin. That day, Michelle left Dr. Natalie's office a different person. The scales of obscurity were lifting from her soul, and Michelle felt perfect peace. Michelle felt love—a love that broke down the final barriers she had kept around herself for so many years. Dr. Natalie and Michelle had opened the second-to-last box—they were so close to reaching the end of this journey. Only two questions remained: Should Michelle open the last box? Could she?

As Michelle prepared to leave, Michelle hugged Dr. Natalie, expressed her caring, and then told her that they had one more box to open. "It's a box that you've brought into the room a few times and that I've refused to open."

"Yes, Michelle, I know. Should we look at that box in our next session?"

"Yes, I think we should, and if possible, I think that session should be tomorrow."

"So do I. See you at 8:00 p.m."

That night Michelle decided to skip sleep and watch a few old movies. She did not want to think about the next box, she did not want to feel it, and she did not want to even attempt to bring it into view. All she wanted to do was escape, and escape she did both through movies and into work.

CHAPTER 17

The Eighth Box: Why Didn't They Protect Me?

In life, as in therapy, if boxes are left unopened, they tend to become even harder to open. Healing is a process that takes time and steps.

MICHELLE EXPERIENCED A SLEEPLESS NIGHT AND THEN A NONPRODUCTIVE day as she waited for her appointment with Dr. Natalie. All day, all Michelle wanted was to be in Dr. Natalie's office. Yet, the last place Michelle wanted to be was in her office. Michelle welcomed the thought of keeping the box bolted shut. Opening this box had the potential to extinguish the only positive memories that had emerged from the darkness she had endured as a child.

In various sessions, Dr. Natalie had gently touched this box and then backed away out of love and concern for Michelle. Dr. Natalie knew that before Michelle opened the box, it was essential for Michelle to be ready to do so. And it had been obvious in previous sessions that Michelle wasn't ready. Each time Dr. Natalie touched the box's locks, both little Michelle and adult Michelle recoiled. This box was to be left alone. It held twisted truths that justified inaction versus action.

Though Michelle wanted to keep this box locked shut, as Michelle gazed at the warm liquid in her teacup at the tea shop, she knew that all boxes had to be opened as part of the therapy process. The healing process had already required many steps and many years, and Michelle didn't want the process to be even more difficult by letting the box seal shut even tighter. Yet, Michelle was still unsure she could handle opening this box. This box's contents consisted of people, not events.

Sadly, the more Michelle stirred her tea, the larger this box grew, to the point that Michelle wasn't sure it could be moved in preparation for unlocking it.

Perhaps, just this once, Michelle could skip her appointment with Dr. Natalie. Dr. Natalie would understand. They could look at this box another time.

No, that was not an option. Waiting for this box to open would intensify Michelle's sadness and prevent sleep. It was time to leave the tea shop and drive to Dr. Natalie's office. Michelle rose, thanked the tea keeper, and drove to Dr. Natalie's office. With each mile, as with each tea stir, the dread increased. By the time Michelle arrived, the weight of this box was unbearable.

As Michelle entered Dr. Natalie's office, Dr. Natalie greeted Michelle with, "Hello, how are you?"

Rather than responding, Michelle selected her seat. "There's a box we need to unlock tonight, Dr. Natalie. It's sealed in the very depths of my soul. In previous sessions, you've touched this box, and I've recoiled. I don't want to open this box. I don't want to consider its contents. But I know it's time."

Dr. Natalie nodded and then said, "Yes, Michelle, we do need to open this box. I also know that this box may have the most distressing content of all. We have time, and I promise you it will be okay to unlock this box and look at its contents. Then, together we'll let it go."

No more words were needed from Dr. Natalie. The flood gates of Michelle's tears opened, and Michelle cried for a long time. The tears allowed the box to enter the room and be placed between them. As Michelle's tears slowed, Dr. Natalie metaphorically handed her the key to the box as she said, "You'll still have your good memories even after we talk about what's in the box. You'll not only have them, but they'll be clearer and easier to hold."

Michelle nodded and then turned the key. "Dr. Natalie, why didn't they protect me? They knew what was being done, but instead of shielding me they turned away and made excuses for others' actions. They could have stopped the abuse, but they didn't. Why?" Anger now mingled with tears, and years of sorrow pressed forward.

"Who, Michelle? Who didn't shelter you? Who's in the box?"

Michelle just shook her head; she couldn't say the words out loud. How could she betray them like this? They'd loved her, and here Michelle was accusing them of not protecting her. "What was wrong with me?"

Again, Dr. Natalie asked, "Who, Michelle? Who should have safeguarded you but didn't? It is time to empty this box."

Hesitantly, Michelle said, "My father and my grandmother and my aunt. They knew what Julie did, and they knew what Victor did, but they turned a blind eye. Do you know how many times my grandmother and aunt would say to me, 'I'm so sorry, but there's nothing we can do'? They feared that Julie would retaliate against my father. They cared more about defending my father, who was an adult, than they did about protecting me. And my father just stood there and never said anything. I do not even know the words to describe how that makes me feel."

Anger started to fill the office as Michelle, for the first time in her life, allowed herself to feel emotions toward those she had always protected and justified. "Dr. Natalie, can it get any worse? Why did they just stand by and let this happen? How could my whole family be so blind? What went wrong, and why was it all aimed at me? Just me! I'm not sure how to feel or even express what I'm thinking right now. Makes me wonder who is more to blame—those who committed the abuse or those who just stood by and let it happen. Every day, Dr. Natalie, every day my life was a living hell, and nobody cared, and no one stopped it, and you wonder why it has taken me so long to face it. Natalie—I mean Dr. Natalie—my dad just stood there in silence! Can you even imagine that? I can't! If anyone even thinks about harming my kids, the protective side of me takes over. Do you know that years later, when I was an adult, my dad said to me, 'You know, your mom treated you like hell, but she taught you to work hard'?"

"What did you say when he said that to you?"

"I said nothing. I was numb. It was almost as if he was justifying the abuse because I developed a great work ethic. Can you image that?"

"No, Michelle, I can't."

"Get this. When I was sixteen, my grandmother on my mom's side of the family said to me, 'You know, if my mother had treated me the way your mother treated you, I would have run away.' I remember wondering where I would have gone. I had no place to go. No one considered me of value. Was I really that broken that no one wanted to defend me?"

Michelle's tears intensified as she finally accepted that even those who'd shown her love didn't protect her. Even Michelle's father had turned his back. Michelle's childhood was a living nightmare with no rescuers. She had to save herself. So, at the age of seventeen, Michelle left home, vowing never to return.

Whispering through tears, Michelle said, "I'm so done with this process. It cuts too deep. For so long, I lived believing it was Auntie Vi's love that sustained me and that there was nothing my father could have done. I believed that he was a victim the same as I was. Parts of those statements are true, and parts of them are a lie. He and others could have taken steps to protect me. Yet they chose not to. Why? Why was I not worth saving? How can a child be so broken that even her grandmothers and beloved aunt looked the other way? Maybe the truth is . . . " Michelle's' voice trembled. "I am not worth loving or protecting. I never have been, and maybe I never will be. I really hate being me sometimes. All I wanted was love. I guess that was too much to ask. I entered this world as a broken baby, grew as a broken child, and now here I sit as an accomplished woman made up of fractured pieces." Words ceased as tears took over.

For a long time, Dr. Natalie allowed Michelle's tears to heal the deep sadness of a lost child and to bring to light the truth that Michelle wasn't broken. Michelle was a survivor. Her family members were the ones who were broken.

"Michelle, I don't know why they didn't save you. They should have, and it was wrong of them not to do so. I do believe your Auntie Vi loved you and that the memories you hold of her love are true. She held you; she told you bedtime stories; she let you be a child, even if only for a few days each year. So, yes, she did love her little Michelle. That doesn't excuse her actions, but it's important you hold on to that love. I believe it was from her that you learned enough about love to be the amazing individual you are today. So many kids wouldn't have ever made it out or been able to achieve the life you have. I think you owe some of your success to Auntie Vi."

As Michelle's tears slowed, she nodded in agreement. Michelle was struggling to verbalize her feelings as her heart accepted truth. Michelle's tears permitted her soul to sift through lies while recognizing the moments of love she did experience as a child. It was the love of a great-aunt for her favorite niece. Michelle had learned that her Auntie Vi's last name meant "giver of light." Auntie Vi had indeed, in a small but significant way, opened Michelle heart to seek light.

Many hours later, after both Michelle's anger and sadness were liberated, Dr. Natalie and Michelle ended their session. With tears in their eyes, they acknowledged the powerful healing that occurred in the office that evening. A trained mentor and guide had assisted a child and an adult to release torment by replacing nightmares with the love that Michelle had known as a child and that was now part of her adult life.

That night, Dr. Natalie's compassion had guided Michelle to understand Auntie Vi's love so that Michelle could trust and feel the love of her children, of Barbara, of Dr. Natalie, of Ivan, and of Joy. Michelle was healing. She was safe. She was loved.

Michelle now held the keys of healing. She no longer needed boxes. The journey of eighteen months, which was only to take a few weeks, had concluded changing both the client and the therapist, leaving both with renewed perspectives of therapy, the human soul's desire to heal, the power of love, the need for human connection, and that it is possible to unlock and empty every box. Michelle's and Dr. Natalie's lives changed as together they replaced darkness with truth, pain with hope, and boxes with light. Michelle had found truth in the opening of each box. Truth that she was worth loving, that she could let others love her, that she loved deeply, that abuse was wrong, and that she no longer needed to run from the past. Also, the truth that surviving her past had helped to create the powerful, beautiful woman who both entered into and left Dr. Natalie's office.

Healing does not come all at once, and for all of us mortals it is a life-long journey we seek daily regardless of what wounds are inflicted, for in healing we love deeper, trust greater, comfort more, hope in life, and place our faith in Christ.

CHAPTER 18

Michelle's Life Outside of Therapy

From each event in life, we can choose to carry darkness or light. Light comes when we accept truth and see the strengths that resulted from darkness. By accepting our strengths, we move from being a victim, to surviving, to being whole.

NOW THAT YOU HAVE READ THE ACCOUNT OF MICHELLE'S AND DR. NATALIE'S unlocking boxes healing journey, it's important to tell you a little about Michelle's life outside the therapy office. After Michelle's high school graduation, she went to live with her Auntie Vi.

Michelle noted one thing her childhood taught her was what she didn't want. As she and her Auntie Vi covered the miles from Auntie Vi's home to the University of Alabama, Michelle started telling the story of life that would be, not the life that had been. She would go to college. She would wear clean clothes. She would live inside. She would be seen. No one would make fun of her. She would retell her life story and no longer know silence.

During her first year at the university, she met Ivan in a pre-law class. Michelle was planning to go to law school because of her experiences with the Future Farmers of America (FFA) during her junior year of high school. She had been selected to attend the state and national FFA conventions. Within FFA Michelle gained insight into her abilities of leadership, which cemented her desire for continued education. As Michelle's education progressed, she decided to switch from studying law to mental health, eventually earning a doctorate in clinical psychology. As she progressed through her education, Michelle was blessed to welcome into her home amazing children. These children helped save Michelle. During the trial-and-error process of raising them she learned the attributes of motherhood.

Over the following years, Michelle would go on to hold many leadership positions, run several companies, continue to serve in her church, and serve on various non-profit and corporate boards. In each facet of her life after leaving her parents' home, Michelle found joy and experienced progress. Although her family had given her much darkness, they had indeed taught her the skill of hard work, independence, and a love for country. Michelle learned to love and serve all around her. She chose to guide with love and understanding. She considered herself content with her life. Yet, as each year of her adult life passed through self-actualization, Michelle wanted more than contentment, which is why she decided to complete the healing journey with Dr. Natalie. At the end, Michelle experienced deeper love and wholeness. Each event in Michelle's life allowed healing to enter in while preparing her for the crescendo work that took place in Dr. Natalie's office.

The work in Dr. Natalie's office helped her increase her positive relationship with her father. She keeps the boundaries she wants with him. Michelle's mother is no longer living. Michelle decided not to share this story with her children, as she desires them to have a positive relationship with their grandfather. Michelle's younger siblings know nothing of her childhood because of the age difference between them, and she doesn't think they need to know.

She now owns her past—it doesn't own her. Michelle decides whether and when to share her odyssey. In healing, the past should be shared only when prompted in an intimate setting, not proclaimed from a pulpit.

Today, Michelle is busier than ever, not because she is running away but because she wants to make a difference in the lives of all those she meets. She wants to pay forward what she received in Dr. Natalie's office. In that office, Michelle opened and unlocked boxes, darkness left, and light entered. She and Dr. Natalie did the hard work together—and, yes, therapy is hard work. Together, they allowed the past to heal, the present to be analyzed, and the future to be considered while focusing on truth. Together, they broke through the silence of the past, allowed silence in the present, and formed a positive client-therapist relationship. This relationship opened the door for difficult discussions and for vulnerability.

For Michelle, the final gift from completing her journey of healing is a deeper relationship with her children and her Savior Jesus Christ. There's no longer a barrier between them and her, and that's a majestic gift. Thus, a great gift of therapy is that one feels loved by those who they choose to be part of their heart family. Michelle no longer holds shame from her past.

Now, I offer you a challenge: Don't give up on therapy. Don't give up on life. Don't give up on Him. There is indeed darkness in this world, but there is so much more light. Expose your wick to those you trust, and they will help you obtain the light and healing you seek. Go find your Dr. Natalie.

EPILOGUE

I WROTE THIS BOOK TO ENCOURAGE OTHERS TO TAKE THEIR PERSONAL healing journeys. As you contemplate Michelle's journey, I once again ask you to not see an abused child but an individual who had the courage to unlock boxes. Healing is a gift all people can receive if they're willing to consider the following:

1. Recognize that healing is a tender mercy that comes when you accept yourself rather than judge yourself. True healing is attainable through the balm of Gilead being skillfully applied by one who has dedicated his or her life to lift, disentangle, encourage, and guide to wholeness those whose childhood experiences created fractured souls and splintered memories. Ultimate healing comes in layers as processed through the purifying power of the Atonement of Jesus Christ.

2. Accept what's missing in your life and avoid making excuses. Healing is not about whether you are or were a victim or a survivor; it is about wholeness.

   The journey of healing begins when individuals realize they seek deeper meaning and completeness in life. For the quest to be effective, it needs to be navigated by a sage mental health guide and committed participant.

3. A true healing quest is difficult but rewarding. Within your soul, you need to know you're ready for the journey and want to change your life. If you have the courage to heal, you will feel different and will see things differently. You can find peace.

   Therapy isn't a process of compulsion but a journey of surrender, as pride yields to the rawness of vulnerability. Vulnerability opens wounded souls to the healing power of love, truth, forgiveness, and acceptance.

4. True healing can't be accomplished alone. Taking the journey alone isn't God's plan. To arrive at the right healing destination, you need to be accompanied by a sage whom you feel connected to and who feels connected to you. People have to go through many difficult things in life but should not have to go through them alone.

5. You may have told yourself during life's journey that emotions are bad, and you may have even tried very hard to turn them off. In reality, emotions are one of the greatest gifts that God has given His children. Emotions are not wrong or right; they just are. It's what you do with them that can be right or wrong. Choose to use them to forgive and to heal. Through allowing yourself to feel and accept your emotions, darkness can be processed, and light can enter in.

    God's crowning gift to His children is the power of feelings and emotions. It is imperative to understand that feelings and emotions are never wrong. Rather, the actions people engage in based on their feelings and emotions can be wrong. Allow yourself to feel your anger, and then act through love. Even anger can be expressed in love.

6. Allow yourself to be vulnerable with a person who you can trust, who holds a professional mental health license, and who has training in the area in which you seek healing. Most individuals don't understand that effective healing happens in and out of the therapy office. Vulnerability is foundational in the remodeling process. Far too often, those who seek mending are unwilling or unable to reach the depths of vulnerable truth.

7. Tell the whole story, no matter how dark you think that truth might be. If you've chosen an appropriate sage to guide you, then truth will be what remains after all the boxes have been opened. Opening boxes might entail remorse, but it doesn't entail shame.

    The process of confession—the telling of one's story—has great healing power. Through confessing, an individual no longer needs to suffer in isolation. Confession invites another human soul in and allows both individuals to be edified and changed. Confession is a foundational, healthy part of therapy, for in the process of telling, burdens are lightened, and truth and love enter in through the help of the healer.

8. As you embark on your healing quest, find your Dr. Natalie. There is power in the therapeutic relationship. Many therapists limit the treatment process by considering the relationship with the client to be insignificant. It isn't. Beautiful gifts are possible if the client feels safe discussing his or her emotions with the therapist and if the therapist understands the sacredness of the therapist-client relationship.

9. Identify a trusted friend you will call when you want to quit the journey and when you want to vent. That friend will be a critical support in the therapy journey. A friend can do things your counselor cannot. A healing quest is best taken with a friend. A friend can offer love and hope while holding up a mirror to see truth. When you decide to embark on the healing quest, reach out and invite someone to talk to you after each session and remind you that you can make it through at least one more session of therapy.

10. A true healing journey will change all, not just part, of your vision. True therapy offers healing to the whole person. Tender, mending mercies are applied to the past, the present, and the future. This process of wholeness reaches the deepest depths and the highest heights, bringing tears of sorrow but also tears of joy.

11. In each session, your therapist will hold up a lit candle, from which you can light your own wick. Your therapist can help you expose your wick, but you have to allow it to ignite.

    Even in the darkest hell, light finds a way in if the wounded soul is willing to light a wick with someone else's candle. The resulting illumination can be shared with others.

12. When you allow silence during therapy sessions, you can find the strength to accept your therapist's nuggets of wisdom, which will enable you to find the key to unlock the box in the room.

    Silence is a meaningful part of healing. Many times, both client and therapist lack the understanding of silence's value and cast it aside, replacing it with constant chatter. Yet, in silence the heart can find the words necessary to heal a broken soul.

13. During the healing journey, your therapist will help you to see your unbrokenness. This view will make it possible for you to survive whatever you're facing.

During the journey of healing, it's imperative to apply the balm of Gilead to the infected areas while elevating that which is untouched.

14. Faith is a critical part of healing. Whatever your faith is, act upon it and allow it to be your foundation as you face the complex journey of healing.

15. In the field of psychology, there are multiple studies regarding spirituality and the healing process. Research indicates that individuals who hold to their own belief system and believe life has a purpose progress through therapy faster and achieve deeper, longer-lasting feelings of peace and contentment than do other individuals who do not see a purpose to life and lack a personal belief system. There are a variety of therapy approaches, so seek to discover which will work best for you. The healing journey is as unique as the person who takes it.

    One major difference between emotional mending and physical mending is that the treatment for emotional healing varies from person to person. When someone breaks a bone, the standard treatment involves setting the bone and putting a cast on it. In cases of emotional injury, one or more treatment modalities can be applied and tailored to the individual's clinical needs. It's ineffective to compare one person's emotional trauma to that of another person. When a client or a therapist compares the client with someone else, the power of healing is shackled.

16. As you begin the right path to healing, you'll discover the need to unlock and open each box. The right therapy relationship will help you open the boxes because you'll trust your guide to help in the unlocking and unpacking process. True healing allows you to empty even the darkest boxes and obtain complete peace.

    In life, as in therapy, if boxes are left unopened, they tend to become even harder to open. Healing is a process that takes time and steps.

17. You'll find great peace as you allow yourself to accept the strengths that your childhood and adult life helped you develop. In healing, it's important that you see not only what was dark but also what was light. Light is indeed truth.

From each event in life, we can choose to carry darkness or light. Light comes when we accept truth and see the strengths that resulted from darkness. By accepting our strengths, we move from being a victim, to surviving, to being whole.

It is my hope that you realize that you can take the journey to heal. It doesn't matter that you're not Michelle and that your therapist isn't Dr. Natalie. What matters is that you can likewise choose to embark on the journey of healing, put in hard work in and out of the therapy office, and experience a great change. Michelle is whole today, and you can be too! May Michelle's story of healing bless your life and empower you to also complete the healing process.

—Christy P. Kane, PhD, PhyD, CMHC

ACKNOWLEDGMENTS

I WANT TO TAKE A MOMENT AND THANK ALL THE THERAPISTS AND CLIENTS who find the strength to participate in the healing process. It is they who encouraged and inspired me to write this book so others might know healing is possible. I also want to thank my mentors along the way who increased and motivated my professional pathway. Most important, I want to thank a daughter who spent far too many hours as my sounding board and personal editor.

ABOUT THE AUTHOR

CHRISTY KANE HOLDS A DOCTORATE DEGREE IN clinical psychology and a master's degree in mental health counseling. She is a sought-after speaker and expert in the field of mental health. Her work focuses on neurological trauma related issues. She is an advisor to schools and corporations across the country in the field of mental health. When not working to help others find hope and healing, she enjoys the outdoors and time with her children.

Scan to visit

https://www.drchristykane.com